365 Days of Prayer for Christian that Bring Calm & Peace

Turn each and every day of your life into a blessing from your God. Ask more, believe more and more in Him and get unlimited blessings through these prayers. One prayer a day and your whole year is successful and soulful!

INTRODUCTION

Your God remembers you every day, every hour and every moment. He keeps maintaining a constant supply of blessings and gifts in your life from His abundant sources. No matter how small they may seem to you, no matter how awkward they may seem at times, remember, as long as you have a last breath in your mouth, you should be grateful to Him.

He gave you breath. The oxygen you inhale is His blessing, and the heart that beats to pump the food (that He gives you and you just ingested) to each and every cell of your body, is His gift to you.

But, do you thank Him every moment? Forget about thanking, do you turn to Him and pray to Him when you are blessed with everything, just to show humbleness unto Him? Of course you may be praying and asking from your "list of wishes" to Him when your life is stuck, when are in a problem, when you feel hopeless, but let me ask you something. Do you need problems, setbacks and disasters in your life to remind you of your Creator? Shouldn't you be remembering your lord at least once every day? Yes your day is busy and you have got lots and lots of work, but if I ask who gave you the blessing of job or business? What if He took your job or business away and you now become unemployed and poor and have nothing to eat or feed your family? Are you unknowingly turning away from Him just because he gave you materialistic stuff to be busy with?

Although some of you might be true devotees of your Lord seeking prayers on a daily basis to send a voice to Him through the skies. Or you might be one of His prodigal servants trying to turn to Him by praying at least once a day from the core of your heart. Whoever you are, this book is designed perfectly for you. It contains 365+ prayers for each day of the year and for special holidays as well. You can start praying from the day you buy this book by just taking out the respective day and month from the book.

The prayers should come directly from your heart while you read them. If you feel that it is only your tongue that is reading the prayer, there is a high likelihood of prayer not getting accepted. Repeat and repeat the prayer until you feel that what you just uttered had some energy component from the heart, until you feel that your soul is somewhat involved it that prayer, until you feel that your inner self believes that the prayer would be accepted. Just one prayer a day and I challenge you that, if you follow it for at least two months, you would see a change in your life and your perception of your God. The gaps between you and Him would be narrowed and your life would be a garden of blessings from your Lord. Amen!

TABLE OF CONTENTS

PART 1

✟

Prayers for the month of January

DAY ONE

Prayer for the beginning of a brand New Year 1

Our God,
as we stand at the beginning of this New Year,
we feel we can face the future
only through Your presence and guidance.
Each of us have our expectations and hopes for the year ahead,
but what it holds for us together with the wisdom
and challenges to meet them rests only in You.
We humbly entrust into Your hands and Your will
everything that will be happening for the coming year.
We seek the assurance of Your unchanging love
in the midst of uncertainties in our lives
as we look ahead to another year.
Amen!

Prayer for the beginning of a brand New Year 2

Lord, please help us to turn only to You
for comfort and stability
when inevitable heartaches and disappointments happen to us.
When faced with temptations and the stubbornness
of the free-will that You have given,
guide us so we may not lose our way to do the right thing
that is pleasing to Your eyes come what may.
Give us the gift of understanding and compassion
in our response towards the injustices and sorrows
that has hurt our world and to the needy and friendless.
Amen!

Prayer for the beginning of a brand New Year 3

O God, Give us a glimpse of what Your plans are for us as You bring together
our nation that has been divided. We thank You O Lord for Your mercy and
goodness in the past year more than we deserve to have. Help us to avoid thinking
presumptuously with regard to the mercies and goodness that You have always
shown in the past, but lead us to make a new covenant with You as we repent and
make You the center and focus this year in our lives.
Amen!

Prayer for the beginning of a brand New Year 4

With this New Year, we are eternally grateful to You as we look forward to the hope
and promise it will bring.
Amen!

Prayer for the beginning of a brand New Year 5

We are grateful for this New Year
And all the promises that it brings.
Start a powerful flame in our hearts
To see Your might and glory
And give us everlasting lives to sing praises to your
matchless name forever,
Amen!

DAY TWO

Lord God,
strengthen me in my weakness
so I would be brave and not fearful.
Help me to be patient and responsible in my daily life.
Help me not to give in to discouragements.
Give me a peaceful spirit oh God
that I may be strengthened in my times of need.
You are my rock and my salvation.
You are my hiding place and my succor in times of trouble.
Lord, I know that You are ever vigilant
to all Your servants who cry out for help.
Our earthly bodies can only be strengthened
when hope is renewed by Your presence.
I am fearless as long as I have You.
You are my God, to whom shall I be afraid?
Your mighty hand is always there to catch me when I fall,
to strengthen me when I fail,
and to comfort me in times of distress.
In You alone rest my strength Lord,
Amen!

DAY THREE

Lord, please help me to stop my borrowing habit. Oftentimes, I borrow even when I have no need for it and not rely on the peace that is in me all along. Help me Lord to enjoy each day's blessings and not worry about tomorrow's uncertainties,
Amen!

DAY FOUR

Lord, please help me to do what I have committed to do. Help me not to become complacent and indifferent, but to live life to the fullest according to Your will. Help me to forget the regrets of the past, but instead feel the anticipation of greater things to come today
and in the future,
Amen!

DAY FIVE

Oh Lord God, through Your never-failing faithfulness, we abide always in the sweetness of the promises of Your living Words wherever we may be. May we be your vessels of hope and rejoicing that could make sorrows and disappointments flee from the world,
Amen!

DAY SIX
Prayer for Epiphany

The star that You, oh God have used to guide the wise men to seek Jesus be given again as guidance to every great and wise leaders of every nation to bring them to their knees and captivate their
thoughts before You,
Amen!

DAY SEVEN

*Loving Heavenly Lord, create a want in me to seek Your presence
at all times of the day, every day independent of special ceremonies and occasions.
May I always praise, revere, and obey Your most holy name
even in the midst of my busiest and troubled moments,
Amen!*

DAY EIGHT

*Most Mighty Lord, help me in controlling my anger if it is provoked today. Lead
me away from the temptation of giving way to it and doing something that I may
regret. Always help me to forget the provocation and readily forgive and make peace
with the person or situation that causes the anger in me, Amen!*

DAY NINE

*Lord, You are the God of love
and I need your sympathy and protection
today, tomorrow and everyday.
Forbid unclean and imaginative thoughts
that cause me sorrow to enter my mind.
Instead gird me with courage and strength
to fight against wallowing in misery
brought about unwanted grief.
Grant me daily happiness
through the grace of Your will,
Amen!*

DAY TEN

Prayers for the Baptism of Christ

*O God, we worship and praise Your
never-ending love and power.
Thank you for the gift of salvation
and the refreshing and inspiring Presence
that You give.
Help us to believe in the infinite possibility
of starting anew every day
through the act of baptism of our Christ.
Lord, have mercy on us always,
Amen!*

DAY ELEVEN

*Lord, our darkest moments always see You stand by with us through your
steadfast love and promises.
Help us to cling to You for support and strength.
Help us to always give thanks and trust in Your everlasting promise
that is three-sided: one coming from the rainbow, one from the sunset sky,
and one from the celestial idea,
Amen!*

DAY TWELVE

*Dear Lord,
help me to remember to protect the reputation of other people
as I do with my own.
Help me to see the good in people
and not to seek out the bad side.
Help me to remember that revenge and deceit
do not bring peace which could only be found in one
who is charitable and happy.
Help me to achieve peace through Your grace,
Amen!*

DAY THIRTEEN

*Oh Lord God, make me remember
that the way I can serve You and learn from You
is to forget about myself.
Grant me the patience to seek Your truth
to prove me worthy to serve You,
Amen!*

DAY FOURTEEN

*Lord God, grant me wisdom to make the right choices
in my daily living and to be responsible for all the decisions
that I have made.
Grant me the inspiration to use my education for a good cause
including the right steps to take to the challenges
that I face every day.
Help my choices make the lives of people around me become happier.
Help me as I grow in my integrity
and develop true and sound values that can also see the true side of evil.
Help me to be more like Jesus through Your wisdom.
Help me to practice discretion in my work choices.
Help me to remember that everything that I do and say
is for Your greater glory and not for mine,
Amen!*

DAY FIFTEEN

*I Praise Your most Holy Name Oh God, giver of life and the promise of life
everlasting. I humbly ask You to guide me to show my devotion to Your powerful
name and make me worthy to live eternally with You,
Amen!*

DAY SIXTEEN

Everlasting God,
help me to bring honor and glory to You through my good works. Help me to
remember that what I sow, I reap.
Make my life one that does not dwell in the accumulation of earthly wealth and
riches for they are temporary.
Grant to me instead a life that is filled with love, patience, and kindness to make my
stay on earth worthy for an everlasting life with You,
Amen!

DAY SEVENTEEN

O God in Heaven,
grant to me the grace of being in control of my life.
Help me to avoid feelings of impatience, enviousness, and jealousy.
Help me not to become the cause of unhappiness
through deeds and words to people around me.
Teach me to be contented with what I have.
Give me a brighter outlook that can be seen in the way I act and talk,
Amen!

DAY EIGHTEEN

Lord God, help me to not to be over-critical and harshly judgmental.
Grant me the grace to be generous in my mercies
especially for people who have the greatest need for it.
May I inspire confidence in others
through acts of forgiveness
and bring them closer to You Lord,
Amen!

DAY NINETEEN

*Lord, help me to embrace what is good and right
that I may serve as a light through my good works
and make people glorify Your holy name,
Amen!*

DAY TWENTY

*Lord and source of my strength,
grant that I may be a solid building
to house all Your good and rightful plans.
Make me aware of everything that I say and do
and help me realize that
doing right is the way to everlasting life,
Amen!*

DAY TWENTY-ONE

*Beloved Creator,
though I feel love for others,
I don't know how to do it.
I don't know the way to show and say it.
I feel joy in the differences that I see in people
But I need Your wisdom Lord in expressing this joy to others.
I want to make a difference in people's lives,
And I want to teach them Your ways of love and sharing
Help me Lord to start my day always with love for others,
Faith in myself that I can do it, through Your loving guidance.
Amen!*

DAY TWENTY-TWO

My Lord, help me to remember
that my work towards Your greater glory
is reflected through a shining bright path,
and not through a dark and lonesome road.
I humbly beg that You light up my path
as I take my daily walk
And make me open up my heart
to Your truth and wisdom,
Amen!

DAY TWENTY-THREE

Dear God,
as I face this brand-new day,
teach me the right way to live it.
Help me to disregard things that are wasteful
and forbid me from the walking the path of indolence and pride.
Help me not to lose sight of Your goals for me,
Amen!

DAY TWENTY-FOUR

My Lord, I pray for renewed energy and courage
to expect joy, happiness, and endurance in my daily life.
Help me Lord to put more importance in the way I live
and not in how I live.
Amen!

DAY TWENTY-FIVE

My Lord, grant that each day
I may become more of You and less of me.
Help me to desire the company of people
that praise and follow Your ways.
May I be influenced by them
that I may serve as inspiration to others
to give glory to You.
Amen!

DAY TWENTY-SIX

Loving Heavenly Lord,
grant me a contented spirit,
free from distractions and pride.
Help me to embrace the precious things in life
such as a strong and unshakeable faith in You.
Help me to forgive quickly
and grant me courage in times of disappointments.
Shed light in my darkest moments
to help me to forget the past
as I move on to the future.
Amen!

DAY TWENTY-SEVEN

Dear Lord,
there are times when I feel miserable and unhappy.
I am sorry for this Lord because I know that there are so many things
that I am blessed with.
Please give my family, my friends, and their families
their daily blessings.
Guide us in all our ways as only You are capable of doing it.
Grant in me an expectant spirit to anticipate
and reciprocate love to You and to other people.
Help me to put my trust in my friends,
but most in You Lord, always,
Amen!

DAY TWENTY-EIGHT

O my Lord, even when I know I need to seek the truth,
I am afraid to do so.
It is because I fear the sacrifices that I have to do.
Please give me the strength to uphold the truth
regardless of the sacrifices.
My strength is in You, Lord,
Amen!

DAY TWENTY-NINE

My loving Lord,
help me to remember to seek out Your guidance
and lean on the promise of 'cool springs'
in times of dry and rough patches in life.
Help me to bow my head
and let You have Your way with me as You will.
You alone know what is in my heart;
You alone know my thoughts, my desires, and my ways.
You have guided my travels
and You alone know my final resting time.
I cannot flee from You for where will I go?
Even if I take flight in the morning
and hide in the deepest part of the ocean,
Your hand will still be there with me.
You have given me free will to lead the life
and walk the direction that I want.

Yet You alone know what works best for me.
In everything Lord You have been with me
and will always be for You know me better than I know myself.

I am weak and always seek Your guidance
in forging my path
remembering that the path is bearable with You by my side.
Grant that Your hand and infinite wisdom
will always be there to guide and show the way,
Amen!

DAY THIRTY

Dear Lord,
You have made me aware
that cruel and deceitful hearts
seldom hear songs of divine love.
Grant in my soul an affinity for the sweetest divine music
that will lead me to walk life's path in harmony and beauty.
As I look around me, I could see that
I also need to share this divine music
with the people around me.
I can see birds flying free
while people are chained to their uninspired lives.
I look with envy at the birds wishing that
I could easily throw away the shackles of life
that binds me
and fly free.
I know Lord that I am capable of doing this.
I ask for guidance and wisdom to do this in my life
and share this with others as well.

You are truly a beneficent God
for giving us sunshine under the gloomy clouds,
You have given us the dazzling colors of the rainbow
as a way of uplifting our spirits
Grant that our eyes will always be open
To glimpse the unexpected small miracles
You give amidst our busy lives,
Amen!

DAY THIRTY-ONE

My just and merciful God,
I bow down on my knees to humbly beg
that You take over my life
and fashion it according to Your laws.
Grant that Your mercy and goodness towards me
should not be wasted.
Grant in me a willing spirit to conform to the works
of thy hands as I patiently and silently
wait for the miracle to happen in my life,
Amen!

PART 2

✟

Prayers for the month of February

DAY ONE

Dear Lord,
let Your Holy love dwell in our hearts
to make us fully live every day.
Reach out and touch us
that we may become one with You
and learn to be thankful
for everything that we see, smell, and taste around us.
Touch our hearts to make us always in awe
of the things that happen to us every day.
Grant in us a thankful heart to appreciate the things
that we have seemed to take for granted,
Amen!

DAY TWO

Prayer on Candlemas

O Lord,
You have commanded women
Who have just given birth
Can become pure again
Through an offer of paired turtle doves or pigeons
Offered in thy name
Make us become Your true devotee
And to make us aware
That You did send Jesus to us,
in fulfillment of a promise
That through Your grace
we may enjoy the salvation
and promises as stated in the gospel,
Amen!

DAY THREE

My Lord and my God,
You have shown that You truly love everything
that you have created.
Creating me in Your likeness
gives me a special bond with You
and I ask for further wisdom
and guidance from You.
I pray that my life will be lived
according to Your plan.
Teach me Your ways Lord
that I may fully understand
and learn compassion and kindness
even through my weaknesses and disabilities.
Grant in me the grace to fully live my life each day
as I grow in maturity through Your strength,
Amen!

DAY FOUR

Teach us Your ways Lord
to give without thinking of the price,
to gladly serve You as You deserved to be served,
to ignore the wounds we get in our battles for life;
to work long and hard and not beg for rest;
to give our best effort without thinking of being rewarded
as long as everything that we do is according to Your will,
Amen!

DAY FIVE

Dear Lord, sow compassion, love, and wisdom
in the hearts of Your people.
Remove them from becoming lawless people
governed by hatred and violence.
Grant in all of us a strong sense of justice
to help those who have unjustifiably suffered,
Amen!

DAY SIX

Our mighty God, make us understand
the importance of our actions
and their consequences.
Inspire us to do well on the opportunities
that open to us.
Grant us a positive attitude
to live each day to the fullest.
Make me a blessing to others,
Amen!

DAY SEVEN

Lord, grant me a willing spirit
to take lessons from others,
not get discouraged easily,
and be steadfast in everything that I do,
Amen!

DAY EIGHT

Lord, You are so great
and Your love is so full
and immeasurable that all the people
of the earth could not fathom
and write about You,
even using ink as many as the oceans,
or using quills made from every blade of grass,
and using the lands of the earth as parchment.
Grant me blessings from your limitless sources
Amen!

DAY NINE

Lord my God,
Instill in me a generous heart
that I may treat others with understanding,
with respect, and generosity
Encourage the best in all of us,
Amen!

DAY TEN

Prayer for Ash Wednesday 1

O Lord, have mercy on me,
Take away my sins,
And fire up the flame of the Holy Spirit in me.
Grant me a heart that feels
Love and adoration for Thee, as I take
Delight in Your words,
To make me follow You forever,
Amen!

Prayer for Ash Wednesday 2

Merciful God,
My heart is small and constricted,
Make it large so You can come in.
Repair it as it is in disrepair,
It does not look pleasing to Your eyes,
And I know that it is so
Yet who shall I run to but You?
For You alone my Lord can clean
Me from my secret vices
And keep me away from other sins.
Amen!

Prayer for Ash Wednesday 3

God in heaven,
We ask for protection from the evil forces
that are always around us.
In this Lenten season,
May our sacrifices find pleasure in Your eyes,
Amen!

Prayer for Ash Wednesday 4

Mighty God,
You are our creator,
You love all Your creation,
And Your heart is always open
To forgive Your servants who
Have gone astray:
Make our hearts penitent and new
As we sorrowfully confess our sins,
And humbly bow before Your mighty presence
Asking for forgiveness
And mercy
Amen!

DAY ELEVEN

*Dear Lord, help us to remember
that every person needs to be respected
and not be 'bullied'.
Help us to treat them as equal to us
in ways that are positive and encouraging.
Amen!.*

DAY TWELVE

*O Lord,
help me to put to good use the talents
You have blessed me with.
Help me to share this blessing to others
in the spirit of generosity, appreciation, and fair play.
May the interests and hobbies that I have been graciously given
be further developed in me
for Your greater glory.
Amen!*

DAY THIRTEEN

*My Lord, give me a generous heart
that could unselfishly think of others
instead of putting myself first.
May this spirit of generosity
inspire others to do the same to me,
Amen!*

DAY FOURTEEN

Prayers for St. Valentine's Day

Lord, grant that the celebrants of
Your martyr, Saint Valentine,
follow in his footsteps strewn with love,
A love that comes deep from the heart,
A love that is pure and true,
And may this true and pure love
Which is taken from Your treasure trove
Of love be shared to others.
Amen!

DAY FIFTEEN

Lord, incline Your ear to my prayer
as I pray for people who have been,
will be or are mistreated unjustly today.
This prayer is also for people who have
never received justice.
Hear my prayer as You make me aware
that I have to show respect
for the dignity of the people I meet today.
Have mercy on me Lord
and hear my prayer as I ask You
to change my heart.
Change also the hearts of people who look down,
despise, and take advantage of other people.
I pray for the abused people
suffering under despotic rule
or defenseless against unfair treatment.
Hear my prayer Lord
and have mercy on all of us.
Amen!

DAY SIXTEEN

Let us pray that we will be given
a discerning heart that may be able to clearly see
the difference between good and evil.
May this prayer make us grow in integrity,
character, and instill good and true values in all of us.
Lord, grant us Your mercy and hear this prayer.
Amen!

DAY SEVENTEEN

Lord, we bow down before Your presence
with hearts full of gratefulness
for the gift of a happy life.
Instill in all of us a spirit of thankfulness
and create in us Lord
a positive attitude always and forever.
Amen!

DAY EIGHTEEN

My Lord, people were cured
from the trap of illnesses through Jesus.
Lame people were able to walk
and seas were controlled which showed us
Your supreme power over nature.
Death was overpowered
through the life and death of Jesus.
Death lost its sting when You showed Your power over it.
We know Lord that everything good will happen
in our life when You hold it in Your hands.
We ask You Lord to take over our life today
and every day as we get rid of all the negative things.
Help us to concentrate in the goodness
that only You can bring.
We know Lord that nothing should separate us
from You, in life, and in death.
Amen!

DAY NINETEEN

Mighty God,
Thank you for the gift of generosity
A gift fit for princes and kings
Which has been named after the gentility or
For people born to wealth
who gives benefits and rewards
To their people
which they sometimes exploit and oppress;
May this gift,
Coming from the bounty of
Your treasured trove Lord
Be used for the good
And benefit the many
through Your grace.
Amen!

DAY TWENTY

Lord, change the hearts of those
who kill and torture and have imprisoned their consciences.
Help us to be true friends to those who are in need.
Help us to make sacrifices willingly
and generously to benefit others.
Amen!

DAY TWENTY-ONE

O my Lord,
as I rise up each morning,
may Your love be like the sun warming my heart.
Lord, you are the creator of light
and I ask that the light inside my heart
will always be as bright as the sun up in the sky.
Amen!

DAY TWENTY-TWO

Our mighty God,
Help us to see the beauty that You have created,
Help us to stop, look, and marvel
At the miracles that You have done.
Help us to overpower our senses
With all this beauty
By breathing in the sounds, sights, and scents
given by another lovely spring day.
I feel Your presence Lord in all that I see.
Make us aware that appreciating
The creations that You have done
Is another way for us to praise Your holy name.
Amen!

DAY TWENTY-THREE

As we rush through our daily lives
Help us to stop and
Take time to smell the flowers,
To seek Your presence
And, in the stillness,
Listen to Your voice.
Grant us the strength to
Bend to Your will as
We bask in Your everlasting love.
Amen!

DAY TWENTY-FOUR

Lord, help us to remember
to give our best even to the smallest task.
Help us to remember that great tasks can be done
in simple and easy ways
because of the power that You have given to all of us.
Amen!

DAY TWENTY-FIVE

Lord God,
we take delight in everything good that happens in us.
Help us to be able to share this good feeling
to others through our words of encouragement, thanks,
and praise more so when it is called for.
We ask Lord, to turn us into better persons
through small changes in our life today and every day.
Amen!

DAY TWENTY-SIX

Lord, we know that there are some people
who discriminate against other people's culture, race, and traditions.
We are aware that this simple dislike
could eventually bloom to a prejudice
that can hate, hurt, and even kill.
Guide us Lord to live a life where
we will think good of people first
before we see the bad side.
Amen!

DAY TWENTY-SEVEN

Who can fight us when God is on our side?
God's love is all encompassing that binds us to Him
in the midst of trials, temptations, and danger.
We cannot be seen as losers or failures
even after going through difficulties.
The power of God's love strengthens and redeems us.
Lord, I try and try not to,
yet I sin again and again.
My mind and eyes tells me that there is a better way,
but still I fall.
Most of the time I am aware of making the wrong choice,
yet I still do it.
I am in despair because of this!
I am only assured to go on
because I know that You will always be with me.
I know that I will become better through Your help.
Please help me Lord, and lift me up to a higher place
where I will always be with You.
You alone are my salvation!
Amen!

DAY TWENTY-EIGHT

Dear God,
help me to be aware of Your presence, always.
Help me to know that You are always with me,
in times of sadness and joy,
and in times of light and darkness.
Instill me with Your Holy Spirit
that I should put my trust in You alone
for great is Your faithfulness!
Your love has always been enduring
and Your words are always true.
Help me as I put my life into Your hands.
Amen!

DAY TWENTY-NINE

Prayer for Leap Day

I shout thunderous hallelujahs to You Lord
as I welcome this Leap Day!
I praise and worship You for your tender mercies,
your unfathomable grace,
nd the countless ways
that You have shown Your love for me!
Amen!

PART 3

✝

Prayers for the month of March

DAY ONE

Mighty God, my cup runs over with the bountiful blessings that You have given to me. Grant me a grateful heart to thank You as I count my blessings. Make me remember that it is not in my place to ask for something that will deprive someone, nor should I be happy with my faith alone. Make me Your instrument as I bring glory to You through my messages and good works to others.
Amen!

DAY TWO

Dear Lord, protect me from my wants and desires. Help me to appreciate the things that I have even when I am driven and restless with discontent and ambition. Rebuke and straighten my life Lord and make me listen to the true whisperings of my soul. Grant me peace and tranquility to make me walk softly through my years even when my path is strewn with bitter and sorrowful memories. Dear Lord, help us to rise above the others, not to be easily led astray, but to seek the path or truth and righteousness. Help us to make our world a better place to live through our righteous and peaceful acts. Help us to think positive and to encourage positive thinking in others through praise for their good works. Lord, help us to tread on the right path. Thank you for faithfully extending a forgiving hand every time we fall.
Amen!

DAY THREE

Gracious Lord, be gracious towards my goals as I humbly beg You to protect me against temptations that come my way. Grant me strength to avoid things that are harmful to me which I am too weak to fight off. Help me to have a clean mind and a strong heart to take over my responsibilities and answer for them as I journey through life.
Amen!

DAY FOUR

Lord, please take the helm of my life and control it as You also bless every small or big effort that I do. Help me to complete my tasks while I am young and strong, and eager instead of waiting when I am weak, old, and feeble. Help me to become a good and faithful servant to
You Lord.
Amen!

DAY FIVE

Gracious God, I have seen how dependent I am on You. I have seen that my life is happier because of You. I am so thankful for the gifts that You have graciously given to me and grant that I should feel the happiness and peace that these gifts bring.
Make me remember Lord that courage, happiness,
and peace can only be achieved by way of the truth.
Amen!

DAY SIX

Lord, thank you for the daily provisions given through Your love for me. Teach me thy ways Lord in sharing the bounty of these blessings to others that are in need. Help me to accept Your will and not mine. Lord, I pray that You provide a way for many people who are burdened by debts and could only see a bleak future. Grant them wisdom Lord to see their way out of this burden. Clear their minds Lord and heed their cry to You for You alone can deliver them from their difficulties. We know that the power that is in You is strong and You have always been faithful and loving to all of us. Set your people free from debts Lord. Make them experience the happiness of a life that is free from debts.
Amen!

DAY SEVEN

Lord, help me to seek the protecting wings of Your love that I may be able to live.
Amen!

DAY EIGHT

Lord, take away this feeling of complacency in me. Help me not to rest in my laurels, but instill inspiration in me to seek greater heights that I am capable of doing. Help me to do the best that I am capable of doing out of my comfort zone. Make me live my life to the fullest through You.
Amen!

DAY NINE

Dear God, I know that the paths that I will walk on will be varied and different. I pray Lord to grant me the strength to go on even when I walk on long fields of care, sorrow, and grief. Help me to see Lord that beyond the fields of sorrow and grief are large fields of peace, joy, and happiness. Help me Lord to overcome any sorrow or bitterness that comes to my heart
as I trust in the promise of hope as soon as the tempest is over.
Amen!

DAY TEN

Lord, help me to be frugal even when I am blessed. Help me not to feel wanting in any situation that I find myself in for You are with me. I am thankful Lord as I rejoice in the showers of blessings supplied through Your love and grace.
Amen!

DAY ELEVEN

Lord, I pray for patience in waiting for better opportunities rather than become too eager and impatient leading to mistakes. Make me remember Lord that a patient heart could be compared to a newly planted tree. For it to bear fruit, it must blossom first and be kissed by the sun. Help me to understand that growing a tree is not an overnight process. Help me Lord to become like a tree, steadfast and patient according to Your will.
Amen!

DAY TWELVE

Lord, through Your graciousness, grant in me a truthful and civil tongue and ways. Help me to express myself in a rightful way that will not offend others. Help me to inspire others to act pleasantly and truthfully. I am aware Lord that this will demand a high sacrifice from me. Yet, I rest on the promise of the special grace that You give to those who bend to Your will and follow where You have walked. Help me to be as forgiving as You Lord. Help me to forgive myself by letting go of my past mistakes and learning from them. Help me to forgive others as quickly as You forgive me.
Amen!

DAY THIRTEEN

Lord, I am so humbled and blessed by Your forgiving heart and endless patience. I know that I have caused You sorrow many times through my acts of rebellion. Yet Lord, You remain steadfast and true to me, always ready to forgive. Grant me the courage and patience to try again and again as You forgive me again and again.
Amen!

DAY FOURTEEN

Merciful God, may I be as merciful to others through words and acts of encouragement when they are in despair. Please help me to rise above prejudice and pride as I extend a loving and kindly hand to those in need.
May this act be pleasing to Your eyes, Lord.
Amen!

DAY FIFTEEN

Lord God, help me to remember to be discerning in my choice of places to live in my search for a better life. Help me to remember that abundance in life is not through a lucrative career. Help me to remember that reverence and integrity of character are far greater assets than material goods.
Amen!

DAY SIXTEEN

Lord, inspire in me a thankful spirit for all the times that You have supported me. Make me remember the happiness that I felt when You felt compassion for me and helped me straighten out my difficulties. Grant the same compassion to me Lord as I also offer a helping hand to people that need it most. I pray Lord that my life can be used to overcome difficulties done with the power of love and sincerity.
Amen!

DAY SEVENTEEN

Almighty God, grant me the vision to see the wonders of Your creation. Where there is darkness, there is also light and where there is light there is also the play of colors. Make me appreciate that shadows in the mountains can lead to a great statement for the light on top of it. Make me see that the rainbow is better highlighted when the sun is shining through them.
Amen!

DAY EIGHTEEN

Prayer on St. Patrick's Day 1

Lord, through Your providence,
Saint Patrick became the apostle of the Irish;
Who led the way for the people of Hibernia,
To mend their ways when they followed
The way of the gentiles and forces of darkness;
May You grant them the privilege
Through their later generations
To be called Your beloved servants
And may this act be done with haste,
to bring them to the path of justice and righteousness.
Amen!

Prayer on St. Patrick's Day 2

Lord God may the apostle of the Irish,
Your servant Patrick,
Through Your compassion,
Bring back those poor souls that have wandered in
Error and darkness,
On to the true knowledge and light
of Your mighty presence.
Grant O Lord that the light of
Everlasting life be given to
those that seek to walk in the light.
Amen!

DAY NINETEEN

Lord, I confess my sins to You. May Your mercy remove any evil thing that dwells in me. Help me from walking the paths to temptation as You give me strength to fight them. Your will be done Lord and grant that I do not stray far from You.
Amen!

DAY TWENTY

Prayer on St. Joseph's Day

O Lord God, creator of heaven and earth,
Who created the law of work for men, grant
Through Thy great mercy, and
Through the life of St. Joseph,
The patron saint of work,
That we may be able to do the work
That You have ordered us to do
That we may be able to get the reward
That You have promised.
Amen!

DAY TWENTY-ONE

Prayer on Palm Sunday

Dear Lord,
People waved palm leaves
When Jesus entered Jerusalem
In honor of His name;
Today, may we praise and glorify
His name worthy of a King
And Prince of Peace
For the mighty works that He has done
And for the salvation from our sins;
We seek His divine ways
As we seek Your approval.
Amen!

DAY TWENTY-TWO

Lord, make me aware of the brightness of dawn after the darkness of night. Take me from the dark place Lord and bring me to the brightness of a new day. My Lord, let Your face shine towards me on this new day as I ask for the gift of patience to see me through it. Make me aware of every action and words I will be doing and saying today. Help me erase any unclean thoughts that come into my mind today. Help me to accomplish a task that I have been putting off. Help me to ignore the desires that will not help me and keep me from enjoying my daily routine.
Amen!

DAY TWENTY-THREE

Almighty God, help me to make the right choices in my life in accordance with Your will. Help me to extend these right choices to the people I meet each day.
Amen!

DAY TWENTY-FOUR

Lord, I thank you for the past and present friendships that You have blessed my life with. Help me Lord to keep these friendships by being a constant, loyal and considerate friend to them. Help me not to lose these important relationships through selfishness and inconsideration.
Amen!

DAY TWENTY-FIVE

Prayer for Maundy Thursday

O beloved God,
Jesus the Christ,
Celebrated the act of communion
with His apostles
In praise and thanks to Your holy name
On the night before He was lifted up to You.
As an act of praise and thanks,
Lord, I beseech You
To listen to this prayer
That I may come closer to Your holy presence.
Amen!

DAY TWENTY-SIX

Prayer for Good Friday

Gracious Lord,
Your most loved Jesus Christ
Was sent to lead us to the right path, and
To make us see what sacrificing for others is;
With this knowledge through the
Example of Jesus Christ,
We ask for guidance and
blessings from You this Good Friday.
Help us see that in sufferings
There is consolation,
In sickness,
there is healing,
And in Your way,
There is hope and salvation even when we die.
Amen!

DAY TWENTY-SEVEN

My Lord, I pray to make me an instrument for enlightening the
suffering and ignorance happening in the world.
I pray for wisdom to uplift the oppressed and set them free to enjoy life. I pray for
the gift of understanding to make me devoted, sympathetic, and
considerate to the needs of others.
I pray for a joyful spirit to give help, service, and comfort to those in need.
I pray for the spirit of generosity to offer a crust of bread to any hungry
person that knocks on my door.
I pray for the feeling of consideration to give help to any hand stretched out for it.
I pray for people suffering from the oft misunderstood disease of depression.
I pray Lord, that through Your graciousness, this disease will be alleviated,
accepted, and cured.
I pray that You strengthen these afflicted people and make them see
that there is always a light at the end of a long, dark tunnel.
I pray for grace and hope for these people and the mental charities
that tirelessly support them.
I pray for people to be touched with understanding, to better promote
and develop cures for mental ailments.
Amen!

DAY TWENTY-EIGHT

Prayers for Easter

All merciful God,
Through the act of water to wash away our sins,
And Christ's redeeming blood,
Our spirit was born anew;
Today as we celebrate
Christ's ascendance to heaven,
Make us remember these blessings,
as the gift of life is renewed in each of us.
Amen!

DAY TWENTY-NINE

Almighty God, help me to keep under my feet the things that will only destroy my happiness. Guide me to clearly see the division between right and wrong to make me live a life free from censure. Teach me thy ways Lord to make me take the right choices according to thy laws.
Amen!

DAY THIRTY

Lord, leave no room for doubts to spring in my heart and mind. Help me to strengthen my faith in You which could be eaten away through carelessness and neglect. Give me the green light to make the right judgment in uncertain times and make me learn to trust them.
Amen!

DAY THIRTY-ONE

Lord, look into my heart and see my desires and the way that I am living my life today. Help me to see the truth of a righteous life. Help me to remember Lord that You will always be with me even when I am friendless and alone. Help me to remember Your countless mercies as I wait for Your compassion towards my loneliness. Help me to have a contented heart for the abundant blessings that You provide, always.
Amen!

PART 4

✝

Prayers for the month of April

DAY ONE

Lord, help us to remember that respect should always be accorded to every person. Bless those that cannot work because of illnesses and the ones that do not have work. Bless my hands Lord as I work for Your greater glory.
Amen!

DAY TWO

Lord, I ask that You open our eyes so I could see visions of things that You want us to see. Give us confidence in every situation we are in as well as faith in Your words that says that You can call each one of us by our names. Help us to be respectful as we accept the individuality of every person. Help us to refrain from judging people just as we also do not want to be judged. Give us a generous spirit to show appreciation and praise for people who have worked hard to reach their goals.
Amen!

DAY THREE

Lord, thank you for the light and hope,
That comes after darkness.
We know that the light is from You,
And not from us,
As you reach out to touch our lives today.
Help us not to waver in our faith,
But to be steadfast in our hearts,
As we accept and hold in
all the love that you bless us with.
Grant us your grace to
Find happiness and peace in
Your love for us
For it is bright and understanding.
Create a hot spark of joy
In our hearts Lord
As we open our eyes
to the vision of your marvelous presence.
Make us feel inspired
To work hard for the good of the many
Leading to a world
which is peaceful to live in.
Amen!

DAY FOUR

Lord, I can face today and tomorrow
For I have you in my life.
Thank you Lord for
Protecting me even when
Oftentimes I place myself in danger.
My life always has
Petty incidents
That cannot be addressed
Philosophically, no matter how hard I try.
Help me Lord,
Through these difficult times
by making my mind steady and true.
Help those who are in the same predicament
As we try to patiently work hard
in spreading your word wherever we may be.
Lord, oftentimes the road is hard and tough,
We feel despair and think that we cannot go on.
Yet, we endure for
We see that the world becomes a better place
when we bring goodness to it.
We pray for strength from you Lord,
To make us go on despite
Of our shortcomings,
As we face many dangers
Along life's paths,
With insurmountable mountains
and only a narrow road through it.
Yet, we rest in your promise
Of showing us the way,
As long as we remain steadfast in

our faith in you.
Lord, we also pray
For those travelers
Who walk the same path as well;
We pray
For your guiding hand as
They face the same dangers,
To bring light
In darkness, and
To bring hope
to overcome fear.
Amen!

DAY FIVE

Lord, make us your peace makers as we build bridges across individuals, concentrating more on the things that can unite us while making us see the wonders of our differences. Lord, we have seen how easy it is to destroy relationships. We pray for the power of the Holy Spirit to be instilled in us so we would be capable of creating loving bonds between different people.
Amen!

DAY SIX

Almighty God, your omniscient powers has blessed us with different abilities and talents. Help us Lord to be able to develop and grow these gifts within us. Make us generous and humble to acknowledge the abilities of other people and give praise when it is due.
Amen!

DAY SEVEN

*Lord, make me victorious over my desires through the strength coming from you.
I find myself in the deepest and darkest depths and I need your guidance Lord to
raise me up as your strength gives me a renewed spirit to struggle fearlessly against
the dark forces pulling me down.
It is only in you Lord that I can find inspiration and understanding.
Amen!*

DAY EIGHT

*Lord, we know that You are the God of peace. We thank you for instilling the spirit
of peace within us which serves as our inspiration for every effort, achievement, and
hope that we do in our lives. Empowered with the spirit of peace, may we sow peace
instead of hate, sympathy in place of suspicion, and care where there is indifference.
Help us to meet the demands of love towards our fellowmen so we may sow the
seeds of peace. Lord, help those who are oppressed and suffering while trying to
make changes in the world to make it a better place to live. Establish your kingdom
of love, peace, and justice Lord to all the people regardless of language and race.
Fill the earth with your glory.
Amen!*

DAY NINE

*Lord, You are God of all the earth and its inhabitants. We pray that we always live
in your mighty presence every day. Help us to tread along the righteous path as we
journey through our lives. Help us to find unity despite differences by giving value
and respect to the others even if we think differently. Help us to find people willing
to help us as much as we want to help them.
Amen!*

DAY TEN

Mighty God, we are aware that life will always have its share of difficulties and problems. We pray for strength and courage to face these times, but not only to our difficulties. We pray that we could still help others even in the midst of our problems. Help us Lord to overcome feelings of bitterness towards situations or people. Give us a loving heart to transcend feelings of hatred, evil thoughts and actions, and bitterness. Make us grow in maturity as we turn problems into opportunities to give a helping hand to others.
Amen!

DAY ELEVEN

Lord, grant me peace to be contented
with things that I am unable to change,
strength to make changes if it is possible,
and wisdom to make the right decision.
Amen!

DAY TWELVE

God, make us remember that we have a responsibility and duty to look out for our fellowmen along with our own rights.
Amen!

DAY THIRTEEN

Lord, we pray for our world peace. We pray for justice to the people that have undergone violence. We pray for you to touch the hearts of people who violate people's rights and make them come to you. Our part of the world is beset by injustice and war. We pray Lord for peace to reign over us.
Lord, unto you nothing is impossible
and we ask for peace, harmony, reconciliation, and justice for all.
We see many challenges ahead of us. Make us remember the power of your love for the messengers that make miracles happen. Where there is injustice, we pray for peace. We pray for miracles to happen today as it did in the past.
Amen!

DAY FOURTEEN

Lord, let my light shine before others that they may see my good works and thoughts and glorify your name. Use me Lord as an instrument for your peace, a voice taking up the cudgels for the weak and oppressed. I am aware that following your ways will be hard and difficult, but I abide in your strength as I do your work.
Amen!

DAY FIFTEEN

Lord, thou art a loving God. I pray that you inspire me with the same divine love which could make me see and inspire the best in other people. I pray for a positive outlook, a generous and welcoming spirit to make others feel important. I pray that I will serve as an inspiration for others to do the same not only to me, but to other people as well.
Amen!

DAY SIXTEEN

Dear God,
I pray that today
You will give me a chance
To do a single thing
As a way
To make the world better
Even for a small thing
Such as a smile,
A praise, or
a word of thanks to inspire someone.
I pray Lord,
To give me this chance
to make this small difference.
I thank you
If you give me any chance
To be able to do this
For I believe in your teachings
Stating that doing good
sheds love and light to the world;
I pray Lord,
For this chance
to do something good today.
Amen!

DAY SEVENTEEN

Stay with me Lord as night falls and darkness surrounds me;
Stay with me Lord as my world falls in times of trouble and friends forsake me;
Help me Lord for I am helpless and stay with me,
For my life is short and quickly snuffed out,
My longings for earthly things pass out together with my achievements,
And all around I see are decay and changes,
But for you Lord, who never changes,
I beg you to stay with me.
Your presence is what I need every second, minute, and hour,
For you alone Lord can protect me against the dangers surrounding me,
You alone can guide me as you stay with me.
Stay with me Lord through good and sad times,
For I have nothing to fear as long as I have you.
I hold no bitterness even for every tear shed,
Nor do I fear the weight of my illness,
For death no longer holds its sting,
when victory over it was won in Calvary.
Stay with me Lord as I triumph over death,
Bring the cross closer to me as I close my eyes,
Light up the path of darkness,
As I follow you to the skies,
For as soon as day breaks,
The sunshine will chase all the dark clouds away.
Stay with me Lord,
in life, and in death, stay with me.
Stay with me Lord
In times of trouble,
Help me to stay with others

when they need me most.
Others may not be able
To understand suffering and pain
as I might try to explain it to them,
For it is only you Lord
And your loving presence that is with me
through sickness and in health.
Lord, grant that I may be able
to bring kindness and light to the world.
My faith in you has made me strong
To make me understand and feel
The sufferings of others,
For I know Lord that it is during
These hours of darkness when
Inner peace descends to my soul.
Amen!

DAY EIGHTEEN

Dear God, grant to me the gifts of understanding, wisdom, and knowledge. Help me to use these gifts to bless someone in return for your greater glory Lord, and never for mine. Grant these gifts to be used for the good, to make me compassionate and caring for the plight of others. Grant these gifts to reconcile warring peoples, to make them see that only by respecting their individualities can bring on peace.
Amen!

DAY NINETEEN

Lord, not all of us will be famous or well-known. Most of us will not be written about. Most of us will not have great achievements. Yet Lord, in our small way we may be loved for making the world a livable place. Help us Lord to find more happiness in giving than in receiving. Help us to be humble in all our ways, to love sincerely, and always to be fair.
Amen!

DAY TWENTY

Precious Lord,
I know that you work with everyone,
Whatever their beliefs and pasts are;
We always talk about your judgment,
But I have seen that people
are the most judgmental.
I pray Lord
For guidance to see what is good in people, and
not to pass judgment.
Help me to keep my own views
To myself, and
to open my mind when I meet a new person.
Amen!

DAY TWENTY-ONE

Lord, I know all the components my body is made of. I know how the cells have their own functions. I know how they all come together to make me function as an individual. I ask Lord, to give me the gift of wonderment, to marvel at the way the mind, the physical body, and the spirit works together. I pray for a spirit hungry for everything that is good. I pray for my physical body to maintain its good health. I pray for a mind that constantly seeks you.
I pray that I will only be at peace when I am with you.
Amen!

DAY TWENTY-TWO

Lord, hear my cry for I weep with sorrow. Cure me Lord for I suffer. Smile on me, Lord for I am always afraid. Lord, you are the God of love and we want to share our life with only you. Help us to share the love that you have blessed us with to others for it is only this way that we can touch you. Bind us in your love, forever.
Amen!

DAY TWENTY-THREE

Prayer for St. George's Day

God in Heaven,
Make us brave like St. George,
To make a stand for your glory and truth,
which we have seen in the ways of Jesus Christ.
Help us to overcome,
through your strength,
things that happen in the world, and
in our lives,
that do not conform to your law of
love and justice.
Help us to welcome the poor,
Set free the captives,
And give the gift of sight to the blind;
Make us free the oppressed, and
Proclaim to all,
glad tidings of your jubilee and favor.
Amen!

DAY TWENTY-FOUR

Magnanimous God,
We thank you for the food,
Plentifully supplied to us each day,
to enjoy and sustain us.
Thank you for showing us
The way to stock our food
As a way to sustain others who
Need it most;
In the midst of plenty,
We remember and pray
For those who cannot enjoy
The nourishment and wonderful
Taste of the food because of
illnesses and other eating disorders.
May you touch their lives and
Nurse them back to health so
They too may be able to
Taste your bountiful blessings.
Amen!

DAY TWENTY-FIVE

Loving God,
I want to offer my life to you;
Take me Lord, as
I dream to become yours
Every minute of every day
Yet..
I know that there's so much to do,
So many people dependent on me,
I need you to teach me Lord
To place the care
Of my life, and
The lives of my loved ones
to you.
Help me to put my trust in you.
Amen!

DAY TWENTY-SIX

Lord, may I be a loving person to all the people that you have entrusted to me. Help me to always show the same consideration, kindness, and love to the people you have blessed me with.
Amen!

DAY TWENTY-SEVEN

Lord, I have always asked for the spirit of courage and determination from you during my times of trouble. Grant me the gift of a peace maker to heal rifts and hostility between people. Grant always that I see the best side in others. I ask also for the removal of everything that is contradictory to your laws to make me an effective person to share about the glory of your love and salvation.
Amen!

DAY TWENTY-EIGHT

Lord, light up my path
And guide me through my ways.
I am your lamb and
You are my shepherd.
I always want to be with you
today, tomorrow and forever,
I know Lord,
That your task is
greater than mine.
I pray that you will
Always make me
Keep you in my sight, and
Not lose sight of your
plans for us.
Let our work here on earth
Be guided and inspired by your light.
Help us to live
Our lives fully,
With our strength
Coming from you
to be able to fulfill your laws.
Amen!

DAY TWENTY-NINE

Almighty God, help me to remember that I am a unique creation. Help me not to
be envious enough to compare myself with other people. Teach me Lord the right
way to make use of the gifts and talents you have blessed me with. Help me to make
full use of them. Help me to inspire others and make them successful. Help me to
ne generous in my praises for others who put their talents to good use. Help me to
appreciate the effort and not the achievement itself.
Amen!

DAY THIRTY

Prayer for St. James the Great Day

O Lord, your good and faithful servant St. James was the chosen one to witness the glory of Jesus' ascension to heaven on Mount Tabor. He was also a witness to the agony of Jesus in Gethsemane. He was chosen because of his generous heart and fervent faith in you. Lord, I pray that you grant me the gift of following closely the steps of St. James. Our life here on earth is full of endless strife and grief. Yet, Lord, we are confident to emerge as victors in our battles against strife and wars through the consolation and strength you bless us with. Help us to become triumphant over the forces of evil and look forward to be blessed in heaven with the victor's crown.

Amen!

PART 5

✝

Prayers for the month of May

DAY ONE

O Lord of wisdom, bless me with a passion to learn, allowing me to better my life and improve my knowledge from this very moment onwards. Do not give it to me through power or might, but by Your spirit, O Lord, so I can learn and pass it to others in need.
You are the source of all wisdom, knowing our needs before we ask through our ignorance. Due to Your compassion on our weaknesses, You give them to us, while in our moments as unworthy men and women we wouldn't dare.
Being blind, we dare not ask.
Amen!

DAY TWO

My God, I know that all I threw out of my life is gone forever. I pray that I can make it up for it with what I have left. Make me deliberate, so I can prove my earnestness. Make me industrious, so I can use everything I have to better my life and spread Your teachings throughout the land.
Amen!

DAY THREE

O God, guide me on Your path, that, when I get old from climbing life's steps, my soul can still perceive the entirety of Your glory. Keep me from judging and looking for faults in others, missing all of their virtues. Stop me from taking measure of other people's lives and let me never neglect to measure my very own life.
Amen!

DAY FOUR

Eternal God, Let me look to the Pilgrims and understand that true faith doesn't come from prayers within my imagination, but within my heart. Help me to pray, granting me the faith I need to struggle for what I would rightfully have.
Amen!

DAY FIVE

Prayer for Ascension of Christ 1

Almighty God, we ask of You that we, believers of our beloved Jesus, that had risen to the skies in this day, may have our spirits dwell among heavenly things.
Amen!

Prayer for Ascension of Christ 2

God in Heaven, our minds were prepared when You took Christ from us on this day, as we watched Him go, and still wait for His return, so we could seek him and follow His lead in His eternal glory. May we follow His steps, wherever he may have gone, so we can find hope in the glory of Jesus the Christ.
Amen!

Prayer for Ascension of Christ 3

Almighty God, we are grateful to Your teachings, we learned to be mindful, especially of our future in the heavenly land where Christ has gone before. Grant us that mindfulness when we reach Your heavenly home, so that we can receive your praise and love.
Amen!

DAY SIX

Beloved God, please remind me that I can't be deceived in thinking I'm near You no matter where I am. Teach me how to get closer to You everyday, until my spirit finally dwells inside You. Save me from being so poor in spirit that I'll have to rely on the spirits of others. Remind me that life itself has a spirit of its own, and I can rely on it anytime I need, for it can be found anywhere, anytime.
Amen!

DAY SEVEN

God, please help me to be positive. Don't let me want to have so much, to be in so many places, that I never find my purpose in life. Remind me that I should strive to accomplish my goals and dreams, no matter how hard they might be; that I need to build my character myself.

Help us to be patient with others even in difficult times; to forgive whatever we find annoying in others for it's not their fault to have them. Help us remember that we should bring good to the world, which is our greater goal. Help us to let go of things of our past that would stop us from making a better future. Help us to forgive others like You forgive us.
Amen!

DAY EIGHT

Almighty God, prepare me for this glorious day, bless this magnificent morning. Let my eyes widen up and see all of its greatness. Help me to start it with the right foot and not be ashamed or feel unworthy of it.
Amen!

DAY NINE

Loving God, let me realize that, if I'm unhappy or discontented with my life, due to its trivialities or untruths, I'm not living it the right way. Help me find my place, where I belong, where I can stand firm and confident.
Amen!

DAY TEN

Heavenly God, let my spirit live always by Your side, and never get lost. Let me be sure that when I'm in great peril, need, or even unto death, You'll always be near me, and You'll also help to ease up my pain.
Amen!

DAY ELEVEN

O generous God, Thank You for all the little blessings that come into our lives, including those we often take for granted, such as a smile given by a friendly stranger, the casual kindness we receive and give back from people we know and meet, the kind words that we hear and return. Let us always give back the kindness we get.
Amen!

DAY TWELVE

Almighty God, help me have positive, ambitious thoughts, and not be content until they are carried to fruition. Help me to get rid of any and everything that might keep me from doing an act of kindness, granting that, by thinking pure thoughts and doing good deeds, I may become helpful and truthful.
Amen!

DAY THIRTEEN

Gracious God, help me to see the truth as You've made it, and not be indifferent to the beauty of Earth and its wonders. Do not allow me to be indolent or mistake it for patient ambition, which my heart needs for its desires, sometimes having it for anxious hours.
Amen!

DAY FOURTEEN

Kind God, please bring to my mind and heart the important things needed in planning and preparing my life. Help me to use my strength today, so I don't waste tomorrow's time by learning something I should have known the very day before.
Amen!

DAY FIFTEEN
Prayer for Pentecost

O dearest God, on this day you opened the minds and hearts throughout the lands, teaching the way of eternal life to everyone. You send Jesus to preach Your words to all races and all regions. Kindly preach us about Your ways and extend Your knowledge until it finally reaches the ends of the world.
Amen!

DAY SIXTEEN

O Almighty God, please help me to look for those who are in need of it. Forgive me for my failures, let me redeem myself for the promises that I could not keep the best way I can. Forgive me, just as You'd help me to forgive my enemies.

I don't want to be known only for power and pride. I want to fight, to exist, for what's helpful and lovely. Let me follow on Your path with the greatest delight, and stop me from straying too far from it, or restrain myself from doing so. Help me to be obedient to Your rules, so I can learn Your truths.
Amen!

DAY SEVENTEEN

O Powerful God, help me keep this day peaceful, knowing that it's very easy to take it away. Let me do my best to defy indolences or dispositions that might make me spoil the peace. Let me, at night, lay down in bed, and rest in content for the great day I am going to have.
Amen!

DAY EIGHTEEN

Almighty God, bless those who brought me into this world through your grace – my beloved parents, and rejoice that it is also You who will judge me when I move on to a better place, being taken by Your hands. May I save Your rich wisdom so I won't be found poor, and may I be worthy enough to receive Your acknowledgement and hear You say, "Well done."

We pray that Your knowledge will vastly spread in this world, and bring peace and justice. We pray for all those working for way less than a minimum wage in poorer nations, so that they can find better opportunities to help their families and take themselves out of poverty.

We will speak of what is right, as taught by You. Bless us with a world made of love and compassion, where poverty and sadness no longer exist.
Amen!

DAY NINETEEN

Tender God, may I spend some time this morning to look at what is the most important thing in my life, and if it's not worthy of You, let me revise my ideals. With Your compassion, let me free my mind and heart from all unworthiness, and fill their empty spaces with important things.
Amen!

DAY TWENTY

Almighty God, I pray that You will aid me in correcting my life today so I can have a better tomorrow. Remind me to be mindful of doing what is right. Grant me the patience and kindness even in sickness or need, and help me to have faith in my salvation under Your eternal, blissful care.
Amen!

DAY TWENTY-ONE

My God in heaven, let me be quiet and patient as I listen to Your words over all others, some of which that might take me away from you. Let me hear Your divine poetry in my joys and sorrows, in my work and leisure. Let me listen to Your voice as often as I can, until I'm familiar with Your ways.
Amen!

DAY TWENTY-TWO

My God, let me know the delight of friendship, which is always responsive and sincere. Stop me from being so conceited, that I will end up having no friends, or become too weak that I end up being too dependent on them. Teach me how to have a good friend and how to be a good one.
Amen!

DAY TWENTY-THREE

Almighty God, bless my morning with alertness, and help me choose the noblest paths for today. Bless me with diligence, and help me ensure that I won't end up being unworthy of this magnificent day.
Amen!

DAY TWENTY-FOUR

My Lord and my Friend, I pray that, with a glad and kind heart, with sincerity in my sympathy, I might become a great, permanent friend, bringing joy and happiness to them, as I learn from Your teachings.
Amen!

DAY TWENTY-FIVE

O God in the Heavens, I pray that You'll help me in not confusing my life with rebellion, but become peaceful through Your guidance. Help me through the complications of everyday, so they can be just as quiet and peaceful. Keep me growing on the right path of life so I can reach towards You, as relentless as I can possibly become.

Help me give good advice to others, teach me how to become a good friend; to be firm whenever needed. Help me to listen to You, for it is only through Your teachings that this world can progress, and then find peace.
Amen!

DAY TWENTY-SIX

O Lord, give me the desire to pray, and teach me how to do it as if You would have my very own needs. Help me to overcome my weaknesses and strengthen me so I have Your approval. May I be reverent and unselfish as I come to You in my prayers.
Amen!

DAY TWENTY-SEVEN

Eternal God, help me realize that no matter what I do in life, whether I am indifferent or faithful, indolent or ambitious, I can never separate myself from You, and that the life You've created is endless. May I do my best to come near You as diligently as I can.
Amen!

DAY TWENTY-EIGHT

Loving God, help me remember that all You've created in the very beginning was beautiful, and given away out of love. I pray that I will be guided to the beautiful things in life and, from them, receive the delight of Your love.

You know us better than ourselves, You know the darkness that resides within our hearts. With Your guidance, however, we can use it to bring goodness to the world. We pray that people can turn their dark thoughts into positive ones, to learn greater restraint and mindfulness.

Help us not to agonise over our weaknesses, but use them as assets to grow. Be with us in our time of need, and help us be with others in their own times of need. You are always there to help us with our pain and suffering we feel to others, even when it's difficult to express it.

Help us to spread Your light and kindness to the world. Make us strong, that even in our darkest hour, our faith in You guides us forward.

From these dark times, with Your light, we know that we can find inner peace, and we pray that You will give us the patience to grow as we move onto the long road.
Amen!

DAY TWENTY-NINE

Lord God, I pray to You for the lives of all who are willing to be led by the truth, and those who are worthy to follow You. I pray that You'll help me stay steadfast, so no one will be led astray by the uncertainty of my path.
Amen!

DAY THIRTY

Tender God, I pray that I won't make my problems and disappointments even bigger than what they should be, but do so to all the joys, privileges and happiness, which should have a bigger place in my heart and soul.
Amen!

DAY THIRTY-ONE

Help us to make use of the gifts given to us.
Let us bring light, and with it, goodness to this world.
Help us to see all of the good paths in our lives as we listen to Your words.
Let us be a blessing to everyone around us.
Let us keep the human conscience alive and fill it with Your light.
Help us to do what's right, regardless of rewards, since the only one that sees us is You, and that's the only thanks we seek.
Help us to forgive and forget the misdeeds or wrongs of others, looking at things and people as they are, not as what they appear to be.
Help us bring more peace and love into this planet, rather than doing it in our own, personal world.
Amen!

PART 6

✝

Prayers for the month of June

DAY ONE

Lord, please, help me calm my mind, so that I can ease my tension with the soothing memories that are within it. Relax my body by breaking the tensions of my muscles and nerves, just so I can relax by Your side. Grant me the calm and the patience of mountains and hills to go through the day, and restore my strength in my sleep with the soothing visions of Your Glory.
Amen!

DAY TWO

O Wise God, teach me how to better appreciate the common things: the beauty around me, the conversations with people, the listening of nature's songs or reading of good books. Teach me how to appreciate giving time to myself to do what I want.
Amen!

DAY THREE

Lord, grant us the sense to know when something is not right, and know what to do about it, like approaching and encouraging someone that is unhappy or even unwell, inviting lonely people to our group and make them feel like they are a part of it, or doing whatever needs to be done without giving in to the indolences and other temptations of life, that might take us away from Your teachings; that we may notice everything that surrounds us, and use it to live a happy, long, positive life at Your side.
Amen!

DAY FOUR

O God, please take away my quick, discriminatory judgement of people. Take away my ego that only sees the negative characteristics within the people I meet. Tell me how to become a man who doesn't think he's better than everybody else. Teach me to be positive even to those individuals who are negative towards me. There are many things I can learn from strangers and many things that they can learn from me, since we are all different. Treating people with the respect they deserve is the first step to get them to treat me the same way.
Amen!

DAY FIVE

O Almighty God, do not let me rush my life away; instead, let me grow slowly and steadily, healthy and well, just like trees do. This way, I will have myself standing with fortitude where I am supposed to be, and thus stopping me from making unnecessary mistakes and growing strong to reach Your light.
Amen!

DAY SIX

Lord, teach me how to use the talents You have given me the best way possible; how to appreciate and value others while being as positive as I can, encouraging and praising them and their own talents whenever possible. Remove my narrow-mindedness about what I think is "success" and "failure", for it is always different from person to person: the failure of one can, or even will be, the very success of another. Remind us to accept people as they are, not as they should be. Eliminating our differences, we can get closer to You and Your peace.
Amen!

DAY SEVEN

God of kindness,
thank You for Your constant presence, for Your teachings on how to share food
between family and friends, how to enjoy parties with them all. Remind us to be
kind to those who are not accepted,
for they might not have a family or friends
to do it for them.
Amen!

DAY EIGHT

O merciful God, You have made us in Your image and likeness, and gave us
happiness and peace in life. To You, the dead do not die, but simply keep on living,
receiving Your love and Your Light as they are even closer to You, so please keep
them safe under Your light and love, granting them the peace and happiness they
deserve for always being faithful to You. Jesus taught us that the ones who mourn
are "blessed", for only those who share a strong bond of love can mourn. Bless this
day with Your Light and warmth as we pray for our lost loved ones.
Amen!

DAY NINE

O gracious God, while taking away the malice and ill will, grant us the firmness, the
kindness and the light from Your wisdom to do the good work we need: to help our
nation grow strong and prosper, to care for those who fight for a better tomorrow,
those who fight to protect their families in distant lands, for widows and orphans
everywhere; to stop unnecessary wars and achieve peace among ourselves, and
spread our example to the world.
Amen!

DAY TEN

God of kindness, allow us to make the world a better place, by taking Your words of kindness and transforming them into actions of goodness. We trust You and your promises, so help us to make the world a better, happier place by making them come to reality. Help us to overcome our sadness and sorrow, bringing us together as a family in joy and happiness. We are all brothers and sisters in Your eyes, so help us unite under Your light, sharing our pain and happiness, giving comfort wherever needed, so we can grow in love and faith.
Amen!

DAY ELEVEN

God our God, You, who calls us all by our names, even in the vastness of the Universe, sent us a guide, a teacher Jesus to our world to live among us in our time of need. He taught us about Your love, and how to live in wonder and appreciate everything around us. Inspire us to live everyday with love and compassion, like Jesus did in His time.
Amen!

DAY TWELVE

Dear Lord, we have faith that You can change the entire world if You so wish. Teach us where need lies and what we can do for it, so the need is no more. We know You reside in the most needy and vulnerable, so lend us Your guiding hand, that we can help them in the best way we can.
Amen!

DAY THIRTEEN

God our God, let what we experience and what we see make us grow in wonder and respect, so we can value and be thankful for everything present in our lives everyday. Let us use Your inspiration to use our positivity and knowledge, our talents and skills, to benefit others and ourselves the most effective and wise way.
Amen!

DAY FOURTEEN

Dear Lord, thank You for our families, even when the difficulties and conflicts arise. You've blessed me with a family and helped me to appreciate all the good things that come out of the relationships within, which strengthen the bonds between us and improve our lives to the fullest. Bless all of those who also have families, so their lives can also improve under Your light.
Bless those too who don't, for you alone are sufficient for us.
Amen!

DAY FIFTEEN

O loving God, Bless all those who are lonely and afraid, help those who won't open themselves to the world. Bless those who are hurting, heal the people who were betrayed by those they loved and trusted. May anyone who has no friends find one in You.
Amen!

DAY SIXTEEN

Dear Lord, help me to shine today; grant me Your help so I can give praise and encouragement to others, while avoiding hurting them with any kind of negative words or actions, that might end up hurting or upsetting them. Help me spread Your love to the world by reflecting Your grace.
Amen!

DAY SEVENTEEN

O wise Lord, Inspire me to have genuine concern and care for others, being as generous to people as they are to me. Give me patience and tolerance with all. Teach me Your ways, so I can be kind and generous towards people. Help me to become positive and cheerful with everyone, so they will have a positive life as I do with You.
Amen!

DAY EIGHTEEN

Praise be to You, merciful God, creator and Lord of everything. The only One we pray for, the only One we ask for, is You, for You are the only one whom we turn to for aid. Help us to stay on Your blessed path and not be led astray by anything. Guide us on the path we should walk onto, the one that You have blessed for all those before us.
Amen!

DAY NINETEEN

Loving God,
thank You for teaching me how to be patient and selfless. Thank You for teaching
me that, though Your path is long and hard, I'm not alone in it, for others walk on it
with me. Thank you for showing me that the end of the path is worth the wait.
Amen!

DAY TWENTY

My Lord,
thank You for Your gifts. You are pleased when we use them well, so teach us how
to use them properly, reaching our full potential, so that we can help others in
the best possible way. Enable us to grow through the power of Your Spirit, so our
faith, imagination, and creativity can help many more than just me, making other
people's lives worthwhile.
Amen!

DAY TWENTY-ONE

My Lord God, may I treat others the same way I would like them to treat me. May
I forgive them as I would like them to forgive me. May I encourage and compliment
everyone the same way I would like to be encouraged. Let me love others the same
way I would like them to love me. Let me give what I have so I can expect the same
in return, regardless of what it is. May I move forward remembering that doing
harmful things to others will harm me even more, for I'd be betraying You, Your
teachings and Your trust. Help us to forgive and forget the bad things on life.
Amen!

DAY TWENTY-TWO

Gracious God, grant me confidence to believe in others and to grow strong, just as You help others in the same way. Help us rise closer to You, and let us carry out Your work as we grow.
Amen!

DAY TWENTY-THREE

Lord, lend me a heart filled with love and thankfulness, so I can appreciate and treasure all the good things and people who are a part of my life. Inspire me each and every day to live a positive life, so that I can help others and, with that, bring out the best in them, as they bring out the best in me.
Amen!

DAY TWENTY-FOUR

Dear Lord, grant us the power of Your Spirit so we can build on what is good, and change what needs to be changed.
We hope to grow strong and faithful so that we can respond to your call, as we, through Your guidance, came to become, and we also pray that we may rightfully receive Your praises throughout our lives,
every single day.
Amen!

DAY TWENTY-FIVE

Almighty God, help us to assist others, to understand what is needed for them to succeed, for sometimes they are misguided and do not know what is the path they need to take. Teach us to praise others,
for that's how their success can grow in this world.
Amen!

DAY TWENTY-SIX

God O God: with Your gifts, we also received responsibilities. Teach us how to act responsibly, give us courage for when we face difficulties. Remind us to be wise with our decisions, for every action we take has a consequence attached to it.

God, we pray for those who are trapped by problems and see no way out of it, feeling only despair with all their debts. Give them courage to face their problems head-on, grant them clarity in their decisions so they can get rid of them, and bless them with faith that You'll help them when they pray for Your aid.
Amen!

DAY TWENTY-SEVEN

Bless our nation, Lord, with Your mercy, and allow justice to prevail through it all. Let Your triumph roam free in our land as we live and fight for freedom. Have compassion as You judge us, and let us stand before You.
Amen!

DAY TWENTY-EIGHT

Inspire us with respect for the human life, from the beginning to the end. Let us be aware that, when one suffers, all of humanity suffers along, so we have a responsibility to care about our own. May we grow with love and compassion in our heats, so we can help those who are unfortunate and needy, and may that lead to a world without pain or needless difficulties.
Amen!

DAY TWENTY-NINE

Prayer for the feast of St Peter and Paul

O Almighty God: as the apostles Peter and Paul glorified You in their honorable deaths, preaching about Your ways and Your wisdom, and teaching by example to Your Church, let it stand firm upon the foundation that is Jesus Christ.
Amen!

DAY THIRTY

Let us pray for all the unfortunate, all the prejudiced, all the abused, and all the victimized people in the world. Let us pray for the people that live of violence, so that they can change their ways towards others, and maybe become more peaceful. Let us pray for ourselves, so when we face evil or negativities, we have the strength to break the seemingly endless cycle of violence, taking responsibility in the way we direct our lives. Let us pray that we do to others the same acts of kindness we want them to return to us.
Amen!

PART 7

✠

Prayers for the month of July

DAY ONE

Heavenly God, save me from the doubts that might lead me to despair. Give my faith a vision of hope. May I be appreciative of my privileges, wherever they are or whatever they might be, while always being conscious of them, for all eternity.
Amen!

DAY TWO

My God, I pray that, when this day ends, my faith stays with me forever. Be with me from the very beginning of it, so I can properly plan it with you included. I pray that You will aid me in staying away from anything that might stop me from reaching You.
Amen!

DAY THREE

Gracious God, I ask You to test my courage once more today, so I can make up for the fear I had the days before. Help me to see that, whenever I waver, my path takes a wrong turn, and when I'm in a temper, all I find is deception.
May I learn self-control.
Amen!

DAY FOUR

Lord and Master of all, I pray that You make me ignore my desires and pass through my prejudices to become the very best that I can be. May I not wish for events that may or may not happen, no matter how far or close at hand they might be, but to be able to do my work today in the best possible way.
Amen!

DAY FIVE

Almighty God, I ask You to fill my days with the desire to do good, and free my heart from envy. Teach me how to love humanity. Help me to be glad of the successes of others, instead of being envious.
Amen!

DAY SIX

Lord of Life, remind me that, to be able to rest, my mind should be free of wretchedness and discontent. Teach me how to relax in those moments, and renew my ambitions with the hope given by Your tranquility.
Amen!

DAY SEVEN

Almighty God, I thank you for the life given to me by Your power. Allow me to take control of my life through its guiding care.
Amen!

DAY EIGHT

My God, take me away from giving harmful speeches. Stop me from becoming a withering spirit, encouraging mistrust. Help me be kind in my words and cultivate kind considerations about life, as it should be.
Amen!

DAY NINE

My God, allow me to appreciate all the wonderful creations of the earth. Give me a keen, discerning eye, so I can recognize the growth of all your precious creations. Let me, throughout my life, love the beautiful things, and choose things that will make my life grow in the most worthy way.
Amen!

DAY TEN

My God, I pray that my sadness and sorrow do not surpass Your grace within my heart. May Your love break through my discouraged soul through Your beams of light, revealing the sincerity of Your promises, so that I can be merry in Your care.
Amen!

DAY ELEVEN

Heavenly God, help me to understand that, before creating the night, You've created the morning, and You'd never create the night without giving us the hope of another morning. Let me be prepared for the next morning as I rest tonight.
Amen!

DAY TWELVE

Spirit of life, I pray that You'll constantly live within me. Help me plan my life with the best means at my disposal,
instead of allowing it to be wasted in idleness or such.
Amen!

DAY THIRTEEN

Gracious God, allow the world to show me Your great gifts, and the peace and power that it freely offers. Don't let me pass by them, having to pay a great price for my indolence and distractions. All thoughts of peace in this world connect to and originate in You.

We ask that You help your people, us, to grow thoughts of love and peace, and to spread and share Your love in this world filled with conflict and despair, so we can change it. Help us spread Your compassion and hope through the world until it's filled with Your wisdom and Your love.
Amen!

DAY FOURTEEN

My God, I pray that I may not be disillusioned by life and its deceptions. Help me to overcome all sorts of difficulties, and grant me the patience needed until I reach Your untroubled path.
Amen!

DAY FIFTEEN

Heavenly God, I pray that I won't be only focusing in the small things of life, making me lose the great things that are supposed to come to my spirit. May my mind and my heart be free to overcome failures and interruptions, and grant me enough vital energy to progress in the path of life.
Amen!

DAY SIXTEEN

Lord God, You know what I am, and You know where I belong. Be merciful and grant me strength, so I won't stay in the darkness through my weaknesses. Grant me Your light, and May I be contented as I find my way with it.

Lord, even though sometimes we cannot see Your light due to clouds being in the way, we all know it's there, shining over us. Let us thank You for the many wonders You've created, let us share Your goodness with everyone. Make us humble and thankful, so that we can see what's beyond the clouds within our hearts.
Amen!

DAY SEVENTEEN

Loving God, grant me the fortitude to overcome the troubles of yesterday and focus on today's hope. Let me be more mindful of my own strength, and less forgetful of Your promises and of my trust. We pray that we earn the strength to do what we need, being led by what's right and what's good, instead of being led by what other people do. Help us to bring peace, justice and prosperity on Earth.

Let us be kind with others and encourage them in their qualities, instead of judging their faults. By doing so, You'll help us on our paths and forgive our own flaws and weaknesses.

Allow us to follow You and receive Your encouragement.
Amen!

DAY EIGHTEEN

Lord God, help me realize that true affection does not mean I should receive something back for what I do. Help me to avoid being selfish and single-minded; and, with my affections, spread peace and happiness to all.
Amen!

DAY NINETEEN

Heavenly God, You have made sympathy divine. May I never think lower of it. Grant that, as You bless and comfort me, I do the same for others, and do any and everything else You'd have me do.
Amen!

DAY TWENTY

Lord of justice, grant me a generous spirit and help me keep my faith if, in this morning, I become influenced to have doubts and be hateful in any way. May I never lower myself to become deceitful or anything similar, and remember that If I let my life go down, I might never have the strength to get it up again.
Amen!

DAY TWENTY-ONE

Eternal God, teach me the value of the gift of life. Help me think about it seriously, and not abuse or neglect it so that it becomes crippled, for it is mine to take care of from the very beginning to the very end of it. I pray that I may care more about the health of my soul than the health of my body.
Amen!

DAY TWENTY-TWO

Gracious God, help me to realize that, even though I may be content to rest with what I possess, I cannot preserve the strength of my spirit unless I share what I own. Let me be passionate towards humanity so, through love, I can give gifts away, and offer my assistance to the needy without wanting anything in return.
Amen!

DAY TWENTY-THREE

Heavenly God, I pray that You grant me a benevolent heart. Don't let me lose sight of what's true, that others have the same needs that I do. Don't allow me, through needless pride or severe egoism, to fail to help or assist someone. May I always be able to selflessly offer my services.
Amen!

DAY TWENTY-FOUR

My God, teach me the value of everything that cannot be owned, handled or seen: those that I cannot take away from anyone. Help me to remember Your commandment: "You shall not steal," and use it wisely in all aspects related to life.
Amen!

DAY TWENTY-FIVE

My God, help me get out of any bad habits I might have gotten myself into. Help me to stop neglecting any good deeds, put me in the right path. Teach me how to reach for Your noble, higher purposes as I search for the real things in life, and remind me not delay for a moment, but start them today.
Amen!

DAY TWENTY-SIX

My Lord, help me to grow into what I can become, instead of allowing me to be happy with the current me. Do not let me create obstacles for myself or search for things that might hurt me or others, but teach me how to be as gentle as I can be kind, as is the path I should truthfully follow.
Amen!

DAY TWENTY-SEVEN

Lord God, may I not become afflicted so I can't see the other blessings You've given me. Protect me against illnesses that can be brought by indulgences, and help me to take better control of my life. Help me understand that, no matter how much I regret the decisions I've made, that alone will never bring my spent life back, even if it might bring forgiveness for the future days of my life.
Amen!

DAY TWENTY-EIGHT

My God, help me to realize that I cannot improve myself until Your truth is deep within my spirit and character. Get rid of all impurities within my heart and intensify my usefulness.

Make this prayer be true in every day of my life:

O Lord, strengthen me in this time of need.
You are my power and my protection;
You are my shelter and my fortitude, a help in troubled times.
I'm aware, God, that You are constantly watching us and helping those in need of You, those whose hearts wait for Your touch.
Even though I grow old, my faith in You revitalizes my strength.
I fear nothing, for You are always with me.
I won't be discouraged or overwhelmed, for You are my God.
I know You'll invigorate and help me, standing by my side with Your just, righteous hand.
Even when I'm afflicted, my Lord, I feel the comfort of Your love over me and dissipate the shadows that take me away from you.
Amen!

DAY TWENTY-NINE

My God, I pray that You make more glad and give me abundant smiles, while stopping my tears from seeping away from my sadness.
Amen!

DAY THIRTY

Lord God, help me to keep inside of my heart life's very own sympathy, that has the power of life added to it. Help me to seek real things, instead of being deceived by those that only pretend to be. May all those who have my companionship, receive the best of it.
Amen!

DAY THIRTY-ONE

Heavenly God, remind me that I am to live my life to the fullest, even though I might travel through its path without any care or direction. May I notice what I'm missing after I wait for some time at the resting places, "For the road goes uphill all the way till the end, and the journey takes a very long time, from the morning to the night."
Amen!

PART 8

✟

Prayers for the month of August

DAY ONE

Lord of life, We thank you for the beauty of all Your creations. We rejoice when we see new life being formed. May we be warm and kind to others, and never cold.
Amen!

DAY TWO

Dear Lord,
Teach us to stop caring too much about problems and be happier.
With laughter, sometimes we can overcome them with ease.
With humor, we can relieve ourselves from some burdens and put things under perspective.
We need to deal with our worries, no matter how real they can be, by not rushing into them.
Grant us all peace through a healthy laughter.
Amen!

DAY THREE

God, I place into your hand all my successes and my failures, and pray that, through Your help, I keep facing the challenges life gives me with unwavering bravery and determination. Help me understand better what are successes and failures by expanding my sight and mind.

Lead me to always trust You and place myself in Your hands. I pray that I stand firm wherever I might go, as I spread Your light and Your work. Sometimes, it might seem incredibly hard, almost impossible to go on, but I have faith that the joy of bringing goodness into the world far surpasses the hardships I need to withstand.

I pray that You always grant us
the fortitude to keep going on, even with our mistakes.
Amen!

DAY FOUR

Lord, You were there since I was in my mother's womb, and I know that You love me for everything that makes me the person I am. Help me change my flaws into opportunities to grow even further. Shine Your light on me, so I can grow to be the person You want me to be. Inspire me to use my talents in the best possible way, so they can benefit as many people as they can in my life. May we all become a blessing for the next person.
Amen!

DAY FIVE

Lord, let me be the carrier of Your peace. Let me give love where hatred lies, let me heal and pardon the injuries and injustices. Help me to bring faith to the doubtful, hope for the despaired. Help me to bring light where darkness reigns, and joy where sadness weeps.

O Divine Master, grant me that, instead of seeking to be consoled, I console instead; understand, instead of trying to be understood; love, instead of seeking it. For we only receive by giving, are pardoned by pardoning; and it is by dying that we reach eternal life.

Sometimes, my love for others is so immense, I don't know where to start with it, how to express it, or even how to. I notice joy in between the differences and oddities of people. Please, teach me, Lord, how to properly express my love so I can make a difference, bringing joy and love to others.

Thank you for all the blessings You've granted upon us, our Supreme Lord.
Amen!

DAY SIX

I am surrounded by love. My family, even though not all the time, sometimes even with a bit of impatience, loves me, just like my friends. Your love, Lord, is vast, powerful, and eternal, and it's hard to measure or understand it. Fill me with Your warmth and comfort, with the knowledge that You are there, holding me in Your hand and simply loving me.

Through Your love, I learned to love others, though it's nowhere as powerful or vast as Yours. It helps me to understand people, to comprehend where our relationship stands, to see their point of view. It reminds me to forgive as I am forgiven, and to not look for their faults. As I accept You as my only Lord, help me to accept other people with such unconditional passion and love.
Amen!

DAY SEVEN

Whenever the times for change come, things become hard to do, and we feel lost, hesitating after every step. Dear Lord, please grant strength to all those who are experiencing such change, so they know You are always by their side. Let them find comfort in Your presence in times of need.

O Lord, I knew You were with me throughout my life, both in the weakest and in the hardest moments, helping me find the strength I never knew I had, offering me Your aid and Your compassion.

Dear Lord, I pray that all those who are experiencing the same thing I did receive Your kind, warm help as well.
Amen!

DAY EIGHT

Dear Lord, Teach us how to treat other people with respect, even when our opinions won't match, or when they richer or poorer than me or anyone else. If our beliefs are extremely different, our cultures and lives, help us understand that we are all deserving of respect, for that's what makes a human dignified.
Amen!

DAY NINE

Lord God, Creator of light, Bless our hearts with Your love at every morning, filling them with Your countless beams of warmth. May You grant our hearts and minds Your light, and shine it to the entire world.

Please, Lord of eternal light, free me from my selfish and lonely attitudes and let me embrace Your warm light. We need it in this world, so that we can spread it across the land, especially by being brave and pursuing Your Spirit.

Dear God, allow me to be brave, so I can yield myself to You entirely.
Amen!

DAY TEN

Lord God, I realized that the ones that can maintain Your beautiful world, the way You'd like it to be are we Your servants. It can only happen, however, with our own decisions. We must choose to abandon hatred and vengeance, stop being judgmental and rigid, all while embracing love, trying to heal all, and grasp a better understanding of one another.

Lord, please grant me the opportunities needed for me to make a change into this world for the better, becoming one of Your agents.
Amen!

DAY ELEVEN

Lord, I will only be able to live once. So allow me to do any acts of kindness for anyone and everything while I'm still here. Do not let me postpone my actions, for when it's too late, I won't have another chance.
Amen!

DAY TWELVE

God our God, You who knows our names and all of our thoughts, no matter how deep they hide within ourselves, stay with us every day, in all of the good times and even in the bad ones. Grant us the power of Your Spirit so we can grow our character, and let us follow the Jesus, so we can better understand values and ideals.
Amen!

DAY THIRTEEN

Lord, teach us how to act with justice, love with tenderness and walk with humility by Your side. Teach us how to spread peace and harmonize the land wherever we may go. Let there be peace in our homes, our land, our hearts and, specially, among everyone in the world.
Amen!

DAY FOURTEEN

God, let us keep our sense of wonder towards all the miracles of life. May all around us take us to You. Let us value and acknowledge what's best in others, so we can bring out even more of it. Do not let the goodness within us die, so we can bring it to all the new life we find.
Amen!

DAY FIFTEEN

Prayer for Assumption of Mary

God in heaven, we rightfully praise You for all the creations You've made, for everything, be it holiness or life, comes from You.
In Your wise plan, the Mother of Christ had risen up in glory so be with Him in heaven.
Let us follow Her example and join Her in endless life, receiving praises from reflecting Your holiness.
Amen!

DAY SIXTEEN

God our God, even though we are grateful for what You declared to be good in this world, we are also aware of the misuse of all You've granted upon us. Our governments spend resources preserving what does not need to be preserved, and pays farmers to vacate land, so that the amount of food produced is reduced – even when people die every day from hunger. We print, on our paper money, the faces and images of great people, yet no one treasures or respects them in any way.

Open our hearts, so that we can be influenced by what's good, and give us inspiration to do the same to others. Let us change what negates Your love, and bless us all so we may work together, growing as brothers and sisters.
Amen!

DAY SEVENTEEN

Dear Lord, bless us with unity in our lives; with our partners, our families and friends that share a part of our lives. Help us to gather even more, creating a unity of spirit that can spread throughout the world.
Amen!

DAY EIGHTEEN

Dear Lord, help me to put my past and future aside, so that I can live the present. Help me to make the best out of all opportunities given to me. Help me to be conscious and reasonable with my thoughts and deeds.
Amen!

DAY NINETEEN

Dear Lord, thank You for all the waiting and Your patience, which is eternal. Let me take another step in my spiritual life and grant me what is needed so I can progress with that. This way, I can help others advance with me, as we walk towards Your eternal peace.
Amen!

DAY TWENTY

Lord, I pray that You kindly bestow me with gifts and talents that can help myself and others. I also pray for Your help into making them flourish, for I know that the path will be hard. I need patience, wisdom and faith in my friendships. May I be as faithful as You are to us.
Amen!

DAY TWENTY-ONE

God, may the human race not be detached from You by disconnecting themselves, while building invisible walls of colors and races, classes and beliefs. Help us to realize we are all made in Your image, and that we need to appreciate ourselves more. We need to be proud to grow from who we are to what we can become.
Amen!

DAY TWENTY-TWO

O Lord! please remember all men and women, both of good and bad wills, but don't remember the suffering they've caused us. Good things come from this suffering, such as our friendships, our loyalties towards others, our humbleness, our unwavering bravery, our kind-hearted generosity and the all of the great hearts that blossom from the darkness, that grows from all the bad things that happened. When You judge them, let the good things that happened after their bad deeds forgive their sins.
Amen!

DAY TWENTY-THREE

Lord, You gave me the time and the place for me to grow, and I need Your help to use them the best, the wisest way possible, so I can live as Your heart desires me to. Remind me to be thankful for all the people You have put into my life, and lead me to a life filled with thankfulness.
Amen!

DAY TWENTY-FOUR

Lord, We bring to You all those who were unjustly imprisoned and tortured. We think of the people that live in fear of discrimination and oppression. We pray that those who commit wrongdoings and always abuse people have a change of heart and mind, becoming good and honorable. May those of us who are free not take it for granted, and be a good influence while teaching how to value one another as brothers and sisters.
Amen!

DAY TWENTY-FIVE

Dear Lord, may my faith grow by leaps and bounds, let my love grow as strongly as it can, and let my heart become as big as it can be. Grant me Your wisdom and let me borrow Your forgiveness so I can bestow it to others. Take me away from the darkness, and into Your light, leaving all my fears behind.
Amen.

DAY TWENTY-SIX

Dear Lord, grant us the vision to see what would happen if we all lived in Your love, if we all worked together to achieve peace and harmony in this world. Let us start it by praying everyday in our communities. We pray that You spread Your peace across the land with all Your warmth, allowing people to unite under You.

We pray for You to bring peace in our communities today. We pledge to You everyone that works for peace and prosperity, trying to relieve the tensions everywhere. We commit to you all those that are just and lawful. We pray that fear will be no more, that the ones who suffer find comfort and support, that our streets and cities find calm. We pray that people may live their own lives in peace. Have mercy as You hear our prayers, O God, now and always.
Amen!

DAY TWENTY-SEVEN

Dear Lord, teach me how to get You in my life and in the things around me, for I'm often not trying to find You. Help me let go of my past and live the present. Help me to become more humble and let go of my ego and my lone pursuits for my own happiness. Help all people trying to seek Your way. I thank You for being always there for me, and I ask You to teach me how to be as patient as You are.
Amen!

DAY TWENTY-EIGHT

Lord, we proclaim that You are our Lord and Saviour, so we offer our daily praise and our thanksgiving to You. Allow us to perceive your constant, wonderful presence in our lives; to be proud to tell everyone how much You do for us, so they see Your warm love and shining light in us.
Amen!

DAY TWENTY-NINE

God our God, Your love for us all and for our world is so immense, that You sent Jesus Christ, to live among us. May he lead us to a peaceful life, and may he teach us how to work well with each other, so that we build Your kingdom in our world. May Your spirit teach us how to unite and how to appreciate all who are different from us.
Amen!

DAY THIRTY

Dear Lord, as I stand before You, in Your grace, don't let me do or say anything that might hurt someone today. Help me to remember that You love me and forgive all of my deeds, no matter how unkind they might be. Teach me as I am Your disciple, and help me remember Your teachings so I can pass it down to others with blessings and thankfulness.
Amen!

DAY THIRTY-ONE

God our God, we ask of You to open our eyes for us to see the beauty of all of Your creations. Inspire us to appreciate all of life's wonders. May everything our eyes see lead us to You.
Amen!

PART 9

✝

Prayers for the month of September

DAY ONE

Lord, we come to Your presence the way You've made us. Please, take away from us everything that lowers ourselves. Grant us Your Spirit's power, so that our perspective and our mindset can flourish, and our viewpoints become more similar to Yours. Help us to keep our positivity, while being appreciative and supportive of others, as we look upon people the same way You do.
Amen!

DAY TWO

Dear Lord, we pray for the poor and those with such difficulties, which can be very damaging and the depth of it can bring severe consequences. In a world filled with wealth, it is astonishing that people struggle to survive over their poverty. We pray for You to relieve them all of such problems.
Amen!

DAY THREE

Tender God; teach me how to be more mindful of what I say, so I don't waste my time with useless thoughts. Teach me how to never speak harsh things, for a bad first impression lasts for a long time. Forgive me for not using my hours well, for my heart and mind surely have a need for them.
Amen!

DAY FOUR

Lord God, grant me the ambition to work. Don't let me be fooled by my own convictions, working in something that might shame me afterwards. Grant me a clear view of what's right and what's wrong. Help me see the same things Your eyes see, so I can follow You in Your path.
Amen!

DAY FIVE

Lord of all, allow me to always love kids. Help me to remember of what I wanted and needed when I was one, and also the aid and neglect that I've received during that time. Grant me the interest needed to help the children today, for they need that to grow strong and happy. Lord, please help me understand that they don't need my charity as much as they need my constant, permanent helping hand.
Amen!

DAY SIX

Almighty God, I regret the wasted hours of my life, filled with recklessness and misjudgement. I ask for Your help so that I can get over them and start living a better, fruitful life.
Amen!

DAY SEVEN

My Creator, guarantee that I'll live my life just as much as I earn the passion to know about it. Help me understand that what I own do not measure my life, just as my body is not the borderline of it. May I be ambitious enough to reach for the high standards that are free for all to pursue.
Amen!

DAY EIGHT

Heavenly God, my heart feels ashamed whenever I think of the little amount I've given away, compared to what You've given me. Help me be more compassionate from this moment onwards by blessing me with Your tenderness, and help me lose my selfishness towards my possessions.
Amen!

DAY NINE

Loving God, allow me to perceive the depths of Your love. Tell me the way to succeed; giving me a hopeful path, should I be troubled by my failures. Do let me sink myself into sorrow, but seek the everyday happiness that brings gratitude to my heart.
Amen!

DAY TEN

My God, I thank You for life and all of its resources. Don't let me be misguided by petty joys and miss eternal happiness. Grant me bravery, so that I can be strong through sicknesses, and so that I won't be disheartened due to disappointments and shame. Keep me in Your will, with constant harmony.
Amen!

DAY ELEVEN

Gracious God, grant me Your wisdom so I can make kind deeds and have kind thoughts. Teach me how to be hospitable, so I can be cordial in my home and grateful in other people's houses. Do not let me temper it for any reason whatsoever, but keep it so I can be genuinely friendly to all.

Dear Lord, bad thoughts and anger come even to the very best of us. Things from any and everywhere can stress our minds, but with Your aid we can overcome such thoughts and become more positive. Help us to mature well, to learn from everything inside us, even though we don't want them there.
Amen!

DAY TWELVE

My Lord, I pray for the passion for labor and for the will to tend to life. Please, make me more ambitious in a good way. Do not let me keep staring at life and doing nothing, while others wait for its surprises. Help me to become more considerate and have more kindness in everything that I do.
Amen!

DAY THIRTEEN

Dear Lord, still our hearts and fill them with your warm, never-ending love, so that we can spread it to our neighbors. Just like You have time to spend with us, help us realize we can also spend it with others.
Amen!

DAY FOURTEEN

Eternal God, forbid me from taking Your place and start judging people all by myself, for that's Your job. My soul renews itself everyday with Your love, and there is no place Your mercy can be hidden from me.
Amen!

DAY FIFTEEN

My Lord, teach me that, even if rain comes today, it helps life with the aid of the Sun. May its influence be gentle and pure to me, as I remember that sadness does not last forever, for it disappears with the coming of joy. May I search for it so it can be mine today.
Amen!

DAY SIXTEEN

O God, many of us ignore the aroma of roses whenever their thorns pierce us. Increase our faith in You and in life itself, so that we won't be disillusioned over mysteries, but simply wait for salvation with all our sincerity.
Amen!

DAY SEVENTEEN

My Lord, remind me that hearts that are kind and hands that are willing were only made possible thanks to Your deep, great love. Grant me the spirit of forgiveness and respect, so that I won't hold injustices and vengeance, but aid others with sympathy and affection.
Amen!

DAY EIGHTEEN

Lord God, my spirit is filled with gratitude for all of the blessings that I received and savored. May I conform to You in regard of my obligations. May I never refuse Your divinity. I pray that my life will be daily blessed by You, and that You'll transform my home into a place filled with kindness and merriness.
Amen!

DAY NINETEEN

Almighty God, help me to amend my mistakes and teach me how to be more mindful of what I accept in my life. May I always have the love needed to aid others, giving them confidence to take better care of themselves and of You.
Amen!

DAY TWENTY

Gracious Lord, don't let me make You regret giving me Your gifts. Grant me Your pity if I fail to appreciate them, for I have betrayed myself way more than I ever betrayed You. Please acknowledge me well, so I can improve myself everyday with the several obligations of life.
Amen!

DAY TWENTY-ONE

Heavenly God,
thank You for my great friends, and for the joy that resides in camaraderie. Grant
me the strength to capture love, and help me to never lose it. May my friends help
me keep myself pure, and to help me live my life as true as possible.
Amen!

DAY TWENTY-TWO

Lord, today and always, grant me the courage so I'll never fear anyone. Grant me
the generosity to never bear ill-will towards anyone. Teach me the ways of treating
others just like I'd like to be treated. Erase violence from my mind, so I never think
or act that way with others, and conquer my evilness with my own goodness.

Lord, teach me how to live my life while being legitimately concerned with others.
Teach me how to express my care, in order to demonstrate to people that they are
valued, loved and acknowledged for who they really are. I pray that You assist me
when I withstand something for a purpose, when accomplishing it appears to be
beyond what I can do. Restore my bravery; give me endless hope and a faith that is
able to hold on until the very end.
Amen!

DAY TWENTY-THREE

Lord God, show my own selfishness to me whenever I take too much and give too
little. Teach me how to be thankful and considerate of everyone who works hard to
give me comfort and joy.
Amen!

DAY TWENTY-FOUR

Gracious God, keep inside of me the happiness and bravery that never finds it whenever I'm filled with tired whispers. Make my lonely time as profitable as it can be with Your peace. Guide me to those who need my sympathy and assistance, so I may help them achieve a tranquil life.
Amen!

DAY TWENTY-FIVE

Gracious Lord, help me have the deference for the holy and pure things, and help my soul to be content in the company of goodness. Help me to remember all of my cherished deeds, so that I won't depend on the help of others to feel fulfilled when my day comes.

Almighty God, I cannot express the greatness of Your power, so help me understand the meaning of it, in order for me to comprehend what You expect from my life. May I never forget that life is endless, for if I do all it has done to grow so far will be lost.
Amen!

DAY TWENTY-SIX

Heavenly God, don't let me spend my entire life judging others while never taking a moment to remember that You are judging me as well. Let me be compassionate towards others, as I'd like You to be towards me.
Amen!

DAY TWENTY-SEVEN

Lord God, don't let me be so conceited that it might interfere in my job, or fill my eyes with hubris and lose it entirely. Teach me to value everything, no matter how small, and help me to acknowledge Your treasures, filling my life with the best that I can get.
Amen!

DAY TWENTY-EIGHT

O Lord, teach me how to pick my pleasures carefully, so that I won't regret jumping into happy moments, for they can never return. May I satiate myself in pleasures that bring me joys, not exhaustion! Help me to maintain my honor, so I can protect others from any kind of harm and still be able to immerse myself into pleasures and into my work.
Amen!

DAY TWENTY-NINE

Heavenly Lord, I pray that I will never pry into Your mysteries as I search for the truth, for I'm the carrier of Your ways. Grant me Your love so it'll guide me into understanding and expanding Your kingdom. May wisdom be brought to me while I serve You and obey Your laws.
Amen!

DAY THIRTY

My Lord, remind me that You have entrusted me to expand Your kingdom, as it is part of my duties. Correct me if I am mistaken in understanding Your ways. Help my mind concentrate well, so that my hands and my heart will be able to do the job You've entrusted me to do.
Amen!

PART 10

✟

Prayers for the month of October

DAY ONE

Almighty God, brighten my life while Summer lasts, so that the winters won't be cold and desolate. May I live in life's realities, so that I can become more calm and energetic, and use them in my restless moments. May I be keen enough to see the conditions that oppose life, and may I have the patience to wait for the truth to spring into my life.
Amen!

DAY TWO

Lord God, help me to become more considerate towards what I give to my friends, and not turn out to criticize what they give to me. Do not let me become a handicap, but a helpful person to everyone that shares my company.
Amen!

DAY THREE

My Creator, may I remind myself that You, after creating the Earth, said it was good. Let me love the aroma and the grace of the flowers You've created to sustain the soul, as well as the herbs and the fruits, which tend to the body. May I renew my gratitude every morning by singing my song of thanksgiving for all the things You've prepared for me in abundance.
Amen!

DAY FOUR

Lord God, I gladden myself in the sanctity of peace. Do not let me force it where malice is already in, but instead help me take care of anything that finds its way into my life. I pray that You come towards me with Your peace if today I'm filled with turmoil, for it has no fear and knows no wrong.

Your peace is known by us, even though it surpasses all comprehension. Please, God, allow more people to feel it, the hidden calm of Your heavenly self. Help those who have turmoil in their lives, bring Your unchanging love into their changing lives, and bring them ease.
Amen!

DAY FIVE

My Lord, I pray that I won't wander around completely disinterested, without any goals, or be drawn into the darkness through hopelessness. Bring me to the light, giving me the vision of cheerful and fruitful days.
Amen!

DAY SIX

Lord God, I pray that, in my life, I won't become poor due to pure indifference, or burden myself with extravagances. I pray that my monetary condition may be maintained by valuable efforts. Don't let me be satisfied with my life when I can still fight to accomplish one of my works.
Amen!

DAY SEVEN

Heavenly Lord, don't let me lose the kindness that I can still take and give away today. I'm grateful for yesterday's memories and tomorrow's hope, as well as thankful for today's wisdom. Allow me to have visions of immortality, so that it'll help me surpass any hardship I may face.
Amen!

DAY EIGHT

Lord God, help me comprehend that I cannot change the truth You've created, lest I want to destroy it in trying to add to it or take away from it. Do not let my plans shadow Your truth, but lead it to Your shining light. Heavenly God, I hope that I can live truthfully, without fearing life or death, so I can live happily as my faith of eternal life is kept.
Amen!

DAY NINE

My Lord, keep my spirit from all greed. Help me trust Your word as I enjoy Your teachings. I pray that I always speak truthfully, and leave the door to my soul open to such truth, so it can always enter whenever it wants to.
Amen!

DAY TEN

Loving Lord, I bless You for Your kindness and tenderness in Your mercy, which is above all. May I trust Your plan and love in every situation, and as I give myself to You, I have faith that You'll grant me the strength I need in order to withstand whatever I have to,
and I believe that You'll tend to me, as You do for everyone.
Amen!

DAY ELEVEN

Almighty God, don't let me enjoy things that will end up in my disappointment. Teach me Your true way. I pray that You'll aid me when I fail, and lead me through disheartening places, so that I can grow to be strong in Your loving protection and be able to progress by myself.
Amen!

DAY TWELVE

My Lord, don't let me watch the sunset today, as I look at life through a mirror that echoes my rights and wrongs, but let me see it as it is, as it is known to anyone who lives to improve it. I pray that my sincerity in seeking the truth proves itself in the days to come, and help me to do good things with it.
Amen!

DAY THIRTEEN

Lord God, I pray that I become deserving of my friends. Don't let me fear when I'm called and need to go, but give me joy,
even when the path I take is dark and lonely.
Amen!

DAY FOURTEEN

Lord God, I ask of You to tell me if I've been making someone else sad by forcing my selfishness into their lives. Help me realize that the perfect gifts come through sacrifices made out of love.
May I be ashamed of myself when I refuse to give it away.
Amen!

DAY FIFTEEN

My Lord, help me to speak and guard Your truth, so that justice can be a continuous influence within my life.
Amen!

DAY SIXTEEN

Almighty God, help me to not waste my time considering and hesitating during these transitory days, but to use them to pursue my dreams in positivity. Remind me that each day is precious, and that I should live them as consistently as possible.
Amen!

DAY SEVENTEEN

O Lord, I pray that I can always be courageous and master my own life, regardless of whether I succeed in my own sacrifices or be successful in the eyes of the world. Dreams, ambitions, sophistries.

It matters who we might become or what we can do one day, if the day is today. With Your help, Lord, we can become what You wanted us to be today, so tell us what You'd have us do, for it's only by making the very best of every single day that we can prepare ourselves for the future.
Amen!

DAY EIGHTEEN

My Lord, do not let me live in what I think is the reality of life, for I can become selfish; instead, let me live in the realities of what's simple. Don't let me seek only those who might return my kindness, but help me brighten the day of any tired friend I might meet along the road.
Amen!

DAY NINETEEN

Loving Lord,
help me to conquer my grief. Don't let depression take over my heart, but help me to open it for the joys life gives away to every single being instead. May I be blessed by my very own happiness
and assist others so they can also possess it.
Amen!

DAY TWENTY

My Lord, clear my eyes so I can understand the meaning of pure living, and thus no be fooled in my work. Don't let me spend hours trying to search for a better job; instead, let me know that I should feel happy doing what I need to do, for it comes with who I am.
Amen!

DAY TWENTY-ONE

Loving Lord, renew the spirit of docility and gentleness within me, if it has faded away, so that I can feel joy again. Help me in trying to make myself happy over my work and duties, for it should be a habit to make myself cheerful at all times. Don't let me lose sight of the glory of Your kingdom.
Amen!

DAY TWENTY-TWO

Lord God, if I complain about what You have not given me, I might be neglecting what You sent. Don't let me think too long about what I've done or might have done, but be grateful for what You expect me to do and become, as well as my efforts to achieve them.
Amen!

DAY TWENTY-THREE

Lord Jehovah, You who judges all of mankind, stop me from doing the same to others and never do it to myself. Don't let me sink into darkness, but take me to the light, where kindness and honesty lies.
Amen!

DAY TWENTY-FOUR

Gracious Lord, don't let me prepare my own equipment and forget about what the ocean can do to it. It can crush my vessel and throw me into the desert, or send it to the rocks and keep me stranded. Help me to prepare for the tides and hard strikes if they arrive, and teach me how to avoid them, so I can sail in calm waters.
Amen!

DAY TWENTY-FIVE

Lord God, don't let my heart become hardened and filled with doubt. Help me to become trustful and have faith in You. May I praise you every single day of my life, as I submit to Your love and Your plans.
Amen!

DAY TWENTY-SIX

Eternal God, I'm grateful for all the magnificent elements that improve each living being's life. I pray that I never stay as a small being, but grow to be a wise and lovely person, qualified for mighty ambitions and accomplishments.
Amen!

DAY TWENTY-SEVEN

My God, grant me the patience to deal with the hardships of life. Help me correct my mistakes, so that they won't end my peace and absorb my strength. Help me to place illumination and hope in my life.
Amen!

DAY TWENTY-EIGHT

My Lord, don't let me stop working even if it looks hard to do today, renew my strength so I can keep going. May the goal of my job be to please You, as well as improve the progress of mankind.
Amen!

DAY TWENTY-NINE

Almighty God, I'm grateful for Your presence when my heart calls out for You in its time of need. I bless Your companionship when You arrive after hearing my praises. I pray that You'll save my heart from being cruel and unhappy, so I can share the songs that I sing to the souls of others.
Amen!

DAY THIRTY

My God, I pray for Your help, so that I won't waste my life with preparing only clothes and aliments for my body.
Amen!

DAY THIRTY-ONE

Dear Lord, help us to put all of our problems and hardships in perspective, while seeing what's actually important, and praise You for everything good You've put in our lives.

Occasionally, changes in life can turn out to be overpowering, and they are unavoidable. Please guide us through these times, for You are always present through our lives.
Amen!

PART 11

✝

Prayers for the month of November

DAY ONE

Prayer for All Saints Day 1

O Lord, your gifts are always bright and magnificent,
Given abundantly to us for life-eternal,
O God, your saints shine radiantly through your glory,
as the martyrs in their victory become noble and honored.
They shine bright with their rich faith,
This bevy of saints in their white robes, as they
Follow you Lord;
The world's power with their evil words are scorned by them,
For they have proved their worth to you Lord
When they sacrificed themselves through
Torments, beatings, chains, and
cruel punishments which has drained their earthly bodies.
In their way of sanctifying your holy name Lord, and
Their deep faith deep in their hearts,
which made them remain steadfast through constancy and patience.
Blessed with your eternal grace,
Help us to eternally receive happiness
As we celebrate together with the martyred saints,
O Lord, we pray,
In your graciousness,
the promise of life everlasting with you in Heaven.
Amen!

Prayer for All Saints Day 2

Lord God in Heaven,
Who has united all of us
Through one heart in fellowship and communion,
We pray to follow in the steps of your holy saints
By living a godly and virtuous life,
That we may enjoy
Life everlasting together
With those who have love you unfailingly.
Amen!

DAY TWO

Prayer for All Souls Day

We beseech you O Lord,
As we bow down our heads in prayer
To seek your infinite mercy
In pardoning the sins that
Your handmaids and servants
Have done through human weakness,
And be gracious to put an end to their sufferings.
Amen!

DAY THREE

Lord, we know that there have been
Countless times when we only think
Of ourselves more than we think of other people;
Make us aware Lord of the plight
Of others through the grace of your Spirit;
Help us to sense unhappy people,
Help us to notice when somebody does not feel right,
Help us to say the right words at the right time,
Help us to think of visiting people who are ill,
Or to say thanks,
Or to praise,
Or to encourage,
Or to convey warmth to a stranger,
Or to listen to others who have a need to talk.
Help us to be sensitive to the needs of people.
Amen!

DAY FOUR

Lord, we thank you for the love,
in spite of our sinfulness.
We pray for others who are crying for your help, and
For those who are in serious trouble and
are afraid of things that will happen to them
because of their sins.
Help them Lord to be able to
Meet other people to guide them
about the consequences of their behaviors.
Help them to become aware of your plans
through the words and guidance of these mentors.
Help them to accept with good grace
any consequence of their actions.
Bless those who feel
Unappreciated and unseen,
Help them not to become angry and bitter,
but to let go of harsh judgments and resentments.
Help them Lord,
Through your love,
To create a change in their hearts and mind,
To be transformed into good and light thoughts,
And bring peace to our troubled world.
Lord, oftentimes we are surrounded by pessimistic people,
Help us not to feel discouraged by this,
But to give us the gift from your everlasting patience,
To only see your lightness and goodness
in every step of our way.
Help us not to answer in anger
To the harsh words and complaints
We hear almost everywhere and every day.

Grant us wisdom instead
To guide people who speak harshly,
To make them see your light in me.
We ask for forgiveness Lord,
If we fail to act in goodness,
and also respond in anger.
Help us to be able to see and
Weigh our actions
On the numerous times that we fail
And try to learn from them.
Amen!

DAY FIVE

Loving God
You have always taught us
To be humble in all our ways,
which is far different from being humiliated;
Rather it is the spirit
That propels us to reach greater heights
To achieve the goals we seek.
Make me aware Lord
Of a humble spirit which can uplift others
That can honor others
in dignity, fitting as a child of God.
Teach us your ways Lord,
To give without thinking of repayment,
To fight justly with no regard for our wounds,
To work hard and not to take the easy way out,
To work for your glory without the thought of a reward,
As long as we do it according to your will.
Amen!

DAY SIX

Lord,
Bless those who grieve,
As they look for comfort
As they feel the absence
Of a loved one
who has been a part of their life.
Comfort them Lord
And make them feel your presence
In the remaining years of their lives
Even when they feel that life is not to be lived,
as soon as the funeral is over.
Help them feel Lord
That life goes on,
To be lived for other people around them.
Help them to bear the pain of loss,
As it is borne by others,
In other places,
that only you are aware of.
Amen!

DAY SEVEN

Lord God in heaven, help us to clearly see the difference between right and wrong. Help us to know that only in following Jesus may we acquire true values and wisdom. We pray the values in the gospels would serve as inspiration to our country's leaders. We pray that they would live lives steeped in responsibility, honesty, sensitive to the needs of their people, strong sense of duty, integrity as they quickly offer their services.
Amen!

DAY EIGHT

Lord, we ask for an open mind to appreciate and value all people, as we focus on what we share than on what makes us different. Help us to distinguish things that are of value rather than ones that do not count. Help us to inspire people through our good works to make people happy and joyful wherever we may be.
Amen!

DAY NINE

Lord, you have made our life rich and abundant in countless ways. We also remember and thankful for the people who have surrounded us with support, love, and care over the years. Help us to make use of the talents that are gifts from you. Help us also to appreciate the talents that you have blessed other people with. Help us to share our talents with others which come from the empowerment of your spirit in all of us.
Amen!

DAY TEN

Lord, giver of life, you know what is in my heart. You alone understand me. You always protect me against all danger that surrounds me. You carefully created me and knew me even when I was still in the womb of my mother. I stand amazed at your creation in me and I thank you for the miracle that has created me. I pray for you to guide me in your path.
Amen!

DAY ELEVEN

Lord, grant that we may live our lives patiently and happily whether we are in good health or ill. We pray for all those that care for the sick and the people who are ill. Help heal those that worry, are afraid, and are sick. We are aware of others who never seem to get well or who are always afflicted with weaknesses and sicknesses. Lord, we pray to give us all your holy presence for we need and yearn for you.
Amen!

DAY TWELVE

O God, give us a vision to see anew all things that you have wondrously created. Help us to feel awe as we look at the stars that are so far away, to the littlest creatures that live near us, to the different people that we meet each day. Help us to be aware that each living creature is important and should be treated as special. Help us to understand that each person is made in your likeness which we need to value and respect.
Amen!

DAY THIRTEEN

Lord God, your faithfulness to us is great as the Bible always say. You have always fulfilled your promises and have never let us down. In the same spirit of your faithfulness to us, grant that we become true and loyal friends to those who trust and love us. Grant Lord our lives will be like a steadfast anchor for people to make them feel secure and welcome all the time. Grant us a generous heart to treat people the same way you treat us. Make our world wider Lord to encompass the world and make us gain more understanding.
Amen!

DAY FOURTEEN

O God, thank you for the gift of people,
which has made our lives richer every time we gather together.
We know that we can do more
If we work together,
much more than working alone.
We pray for the lonely people,
Grant them companionship too.
May them aware that they never
Should feel lonely,
for you are always with them.
Help us remember to
Extend a friendly hand to those who are lonely.
There will be times
when we too will feel lonely Lord,
make us remember that you are
always there,
always reachable,
to help us stop the flood
of loneliness from drowning us.
Amen!

DAY FIFTEEN

O God, each day brings to us different challenges and hardships. By the grace of your supreme powers, empower us with the determination and courage to face them all. Teach us to be the source of inspiration for others to have the same courage and determination. Help us to look positively at every situation as we travel along life's paths. Save us from danger as you light up our way.
Amen!

DAY SIXTEEN

Lord, the gift of good memory comes from you,
Where we can remember things of the past,
Up to the present,
which makes us remember faces,
as well as memorize lovely poems,
give us find a way out
if we become lost, and,
from an inexhaustible supply,
dig up an array of old and new memories.
Teach me Lord,
The things I have to remember and value,
The things I have to forget as I forgive,
The tiniest kindnesses I have experienced, and
The way that you have known me
through your endless graciousness.
Amen!

DAY SEVENTEEN

Lord, hear my prayer for the world's innocent and the weak.
Our society is still unfair and unequal,
with too many poverty-stricken people.
Lord I pray for those who have the
Power and capability
To be blessed with wisdom
To give protection to those who are powerless.
Grant help o God to
People with learning disabilities,
Old people,
Terminally ill people, and
people who are sick and ailing.
Grant these people
Empathy
Just like Jesus Christ
Who always in sympathy
with the sick and poor.
Amen!

DAY EIGHTEEN

O God, empower us with your Holy Spirit to see and feel love the same love for
people that has made you love them. Help us to encourage the best in people as we
see all the positive things about them. We know Lord that this will be hard for us to
do even when it is easy for us to say. We ask for your inspiration and help to make
us live the way you want us to live.
Amen!

DAY NINETEEN

O God, thank you for people who may live a long distance from me, yet has made a big difference in my life. Thank you for the gifts from people who live nearer who have also helped to make my life better. Thank you for making me feel the respect and appreciation for everyone that has become a part of my life.
Amen!

DAY TWENTY

Lord, create in me a welcoming and generous heart even to those people that do not agree with us. Make us aware that the respect we expect from others can only be achieved if we show the same to them. Help us not to be proud and make us feel more important than other people. Help us not to be patronizing to the others. Grant us an open mind Lord to humbly accept lessons from other people. Grant us a generous heart to share what we have to others as well. Grant us the grace to learn equally from each other to become worthy to be called your beloved servants.
Amen!

DAY TWENTY-ONE

Lord Almighty, teach us to manage the resources you have abundantly blessed us. Help us to manage our personal riches and the natural riches we see in the world. Keep us away from avariciousness and selfishness. Make us value even the simple things you have given. Help us not to take these riches for granted. Help us to conserve and care for the riches given to us.
Amen!

DAY TWENTY-TWO

Dear Lord,
Open my eyes to the beauty of the world, and
Fill my heart with thankfulness.
Oftentimes in the morning,
As I take a walk
I stand in awe at the creation of a tree,
Or hear the sweet notes sang by a bird.
Make us aware
Of your presence in everything
You have created and marvel
At the vision of falling leaves,
or the beauty of a beetle's shiny shell.
Help us to appreciate the beauty of the world
As we become advocates of injustice, and
become your worthy followers.
Amen!

DAY TWENTY-THREE

Lord, you know me more than I know myself. For this I am so thankful. I am
thankful for the gift of insight as I discover more of myself. Grant to make me a
better person than I suppose I am capable of. Forgive me for my sins committed
even when they are unseen by others.
Amen!

DAY TWENTY-FOUR

God our creator,
Everything that exists
are wrought by your loving hands.
The fly who spreads its wings
And takes its rest on my chair's armrest,
basking in the warm sunshine of spring.
The watchful child-like innocence
Of a dog as it tilts its head,
The magnificence of the redwoods
With leaves fanning out in the same breeze
cooling my own skin.
Make me remember,
And appreciate the bond
With all your creation
As I show my respect to them.
Amen!

DAY TWENTY-FIVE

O God,
Help us through our difficult times
and we humbly pray for our leaders
and nation especially for Your people
who seek to bring justice and peace
to our troubled world.
We humbly ask for Your protection
towards our armed forces as we feel thankful to
You for making them commit to defend us
even at the cost of their lives
so that we may freely live.
Make Your presence be felt by their families
through Your compassion and love for them.
Amen!

DAY TWENTY-SIX

Lord God, the foundation of my life will be stronger when it is built on you. Make my life an open door where everyone who enters is welcomed and respected. Erect no walls around my life to discourage anyone to enter. Make me value every sister and brother as we build your kingdom on earth together. Make me forgiving and generous to people who hurt me. Make me as forgiving and generous as you are to me. Protect me from danger through the mighty shield of your everlasting love.
Amen!

DAY TWENTY-SEVEN
Prayer for Advent

Lord, people's hearts were prepared
In the wilderness of Jordan
Through a promise,
foretelling the birth of Jesus Christ.
Forgive me my sins
As we listen to His words.
Help me to clearly
See the righteous path,
To live right,
To speak right
Amen!

DAY TWENTY-EIGHT

Our generous God,
We thank you for the
Gift of hospitality,
A most sacred and ancient tradition
of the world.
Grant this home
A welcoming spirit
to all who cross its doors.
Grant me the spirit of hospitality
To welcome all who step in,
For they are, like me,
guests of the earth, and
should act as hosts to each other.
Amen!

DAY TWENTY-NINE

Dear God,
We always need your strength and support
As we live our lives.
We need your presence
Every time we become afraid,
or when life takes a wrong turn.
I give thanks for the times
Of help
On hard days, and
on painful times.
I thank you for the grace
Felt during times
When I made mistakes and
Owned it without putting
the blame on others.
Thank you for the
Gift of understanding in
Times when things do not work out
As I want them to.
Grant me the gifts of
Resignation and humbleness
To accept things as they are.
Amen!

DAY THIRTY

Lord,
Your grace alone
can make me stand.
Let this day start and end
Without a harsh word
spoken to hurt others.
Make me aware of
Your everlasting love to me, and
Your forgiveness
In everything that I say and do,
No matter how unkind it could often be.
Make it possible Lord
For me to become a loving disciple
Following your laws,
Giving thanks,
As I share my blessings with others.
Amen!

PART 12

✚

Prayers for the month of December

DAY ONE

Dear Lord,
Open my eyes to the wonder of the world surrounding us.
Make us remember the sights and sounds of
This lovely day,
As we stand still, look, and feel
the beauty that you have wrought for us.
Lord, your creation
Speaks and shows your glory.
Help us to appreciate them and
The opportunities you open to us
Every day
Leading us to stand in awe,
praise, and thankfulness.
Amen!

DAY TWO

O Lord, use my eyes to see and wonder at your glorious creation. Open our hearts, eyes, and minds to put importance and thankfulness to people you have blessed us with. Give me a discerning eye to quickly see when people are undergoing hard times. Make us see everything as you want us to perceive things to be.
Amen!

DAY THREE

Lord, we offer this prayer for those who are in the throes of death or for those who are mortally ill. Grant a comforting hand to them as you did the same to Jesus Christ when He was on the cross. We ask that you give comfort and peace to the minds and hearts of people who are on the threshold of death.
Amen!

DAY FOUR

O God, I have a thirst for knowledge even when I am aware in the vastness of things I do not know. Grant me understanding and wisdom in my quest for knowledge. I am thankful Lord for the countless men and women who have made my life better through their blessings of understanding and knowledge. I ask Lord to do the same to me. I ask that the understanding and wisdom given to me through knowledge will also be for the greater benefit of people.
Amen!

DAY FIVE

Lord, thank you for the 'riches' blessed to me. Thank you for the wonderful memories that I will treasure forever. Thank you for the wonderful people you have surrounded me with. Thank you for every good thing that has happened to me over the years. Help me to remember, be aware, and appreciate all these 'riches' abundantly given to me. Help me to remember to make others feel as important as you have always made me feel.
Amen!

DAY SIX

O God,
Help us to remember to put our hope and trust in your words.
You have always been there to catch me when I fall, and
Soften the blow of disappointments,
Every time they happen.
Oftentimes I fail to have the courage
To take advantage of opportunities you send my way.
Yet, you are still there with me even when
I am not worthy.
You have always guided and helped me along the way,
Providing a safety net every single time I fail.
Grant in us Lord a positive outlook
to see the good even in hard times.
Help us to remember
That life's path goes in different routes,
But faith, strength, and hope
Will always come from you
To those who cry out for help.
Amen!

DAY SEVEN

Lord, I offer my mundane and ordinary life to you every day. Help me gain, through
your Holy Spirit a positive outlook to see the best in situations and people. Help me
to make an ordinary day an extraordinary one. Help me to go the extra mile for
someone or for a situation even when it seems to be an ordinary day. Lord I offer
this prayer in earnest like burnt offerings of olden times.
Amen!

DAY EIGHT

O God, make me remember as I look at the largeness of the stars and planets to the littlest of your living creatures, to feel amazed. Make me remember to give thanks for all that you have created.
Amen!

DAY NINE

Lord, give us the gift of discernment to tell the difference between the things that count and those that should be disregarded. Help us remember to use our talents and our time according to your will. Help us to recognize opportunities you gave us as a way to use our talents and abilities for your greater glory.
Amen!

DAY TEN

O God, I keep chained inside me a creature,
That manifests itself
Every time I am fatigued, bitter,
Every time things do not go my way,
Every time I lose patience, become cruel, and
every time when I become disrespectful of others.
Grant Lord a blessing to this hidden creature
which can only receive a transformation,
through your everlasting love and understanding.
I want to follow your ways Lord,
But I fail every time.
Forgive my sins, and
show me the righteous path,
so I could along with you.
I rest in the fulfilment of your promise,
As hope is reborn in my heart,
and my lips offer you praise. Mighty God,
You created the earth and the heavens,
You alone know what is inside our hearts.
Help us remember of your presence
in all things that we think and act on.
Help us remember not to take for granted
The sins that we secretly do
but always to confess them in your mighty presence.
Help us to press on despite our failures,
As you keep alive the light of our conscience
In all of us,
To make us embrace what is good,
To forego success when it means
Giving up our integrity, and
To do what is always right,
Even when no one is there
to see our good deeds.
Amen!

DAY ELEVEN

O God, hear our prayer for those who will be retiring from their workplace and for those who will start on a new job. We also pray for the emergency services as they respond in top speeds to rescue missions on air, land, and water. We pray for people who will be moving out to a new area to live. We pray for the safety of people involved in transporting prisoners to or from prison. We pray for people who will be admitted to hospitals. We pray to safely guide young people as they travel to universities, schools, and colleges. We pray for people who have gotten lost as they travel life's path. We pray for those who are mortally ill and dying to make their final life journey serene and peaceful. We ask for you to bless all these people today Lord.
Amen!

DAY TWELVE

Dear Lord, help us please when we get stuck in a rut.
Oftentimes it is in our minds which form an obstacle.
We think the way is hard and difficult.
Make us remember to clearly see the path you have laid out for us,
So we may overcome the obstacles and draw nearer to you.
We are aware that you are always with us and our fears are unfounded.
Help those who are imprisoned by evil habits,
To learn to live in the present,
To anticipate their future,
As they try to forget their past.
We pray for courage and strength
For people who need it most,
For those who are faced with danger,
For those who willingly risk their lives for others,
For those who needs to make crucial decisions,
For those who are mortally ill,
For those who are tortured and persecuted.
Grant to them Lord the power of being courageous.
Amen!

DAY THIRTEEN

Lord, your love for us is endless.
The fount of your mercies is unquenchable.
Your understanding and vision for man
is beyond our understanding.
Lord, make us a part of the greater things
You have planned for all of us,
Make us a part of your visions for the future.
Amen!

DAY FOURTEEN

I know Lord that all the good things
That has happened in my life
Comes from you;
Help me pull myself
Up from a sinful life,
Where I most often dwell,
And reach out for a brand new life,
filled with your grace and mercy.
Make me ready to enter your kingdom.
Grant me your grace and mercy Lord.
Amen!

DAY FIFTEEN

Lord, grant no impediments should ever block our human family. Help us to disregard race, class, color or religion. We know Lord that all of us are made in your likeness and image. Help us to appreciate different races of people as we bond together in our differences and recognize what we are and what our mission on earth is. Make Jesus our center focus as we try to live as one family, brothers, and sisters in the Lord.
Amen!

DAY SIXTEEN

Mighty God, when we look
At our universe and see the countless stars,
And the numerous galaxies,
We are humbled in the presence of their magnificence.
Yet, incredibly, we are also your creations,
And worthy to be made a part of earth.
Help us to be humble,
And not dwell on our self-importance,
But rather dwell more in
Thankfulness for the shared
Joy with our brothers and sisters
As we enjoy this priceless and free gift.
Amen!

DAY SEVENTEEN

Lord in Heaven, give me a generous heart to understand the actions and attitudes of other people. Help me to quickly forgive even when it is not easy to do. Help me to remember that ignoring the wrong that has happened is different from forgiveness. Help me to be generous in forgiving someone as you always generously forgive me all the time Lord.
Amen!

DAY EIGHTEEN

Lord, people with problems
Seek out answers
Which they oftentimes
Deal with through drug use.
Problems can be hard
That leads to frustration and
Depression if we cannot resolve it.
Relying on our strength
In trying to make crucial decisions
Makes us give up after we are run ragged.
Lord, this prayer is for
Those who try to solve
Their problems
With the use of drugs
As their way of fighting off
the pain of loneliness and pain of feeling unloved.
Lord, we pray for your everlasting love
As we pray for these troubled souls,
That in your loving arms
They will feel the warmth of your love for them.
Lord, our prayer is also
For those who have addictions of all kinds.
Some may have been rehabilitated,
Yet, there are others that deny it.
Lord, we know that
In your infinite wisdom,
Nothing can hide from you.
We pray for these people
To help them acknowledge
Their problems as they take
a positive step.

We ask Lord to help them
in their long hard climb to recovery.
Grant courage
To those who have tried,
but still failed.
Give them strength to hurdle over
The difficult obstacles in their journey
to wellness and health.
Amen!

DAY NINETEEN

O God, you have heard my cries.
You have heard how impatient I can be
with my complaints.
When I am far from you,
I become afraid.
Help me Lord to go back to you.
Help me to remember not
Only my wants,
but more of your will.
I thank you Lord for
The abundant blessings you have given,
And the love I feel when I am in your presence.
Amen!

DAY TWENTY

Lord, make us aware that the gifts of talent that you have blessed us come with
responsibilities. Help us to fulfil our earthly duties to you as we respect our fellow
men as we also expect respect from them.
Amen!

DAY TWENTY-ONE

*O Creator in heavens, you are our God for all eternity. Help us to remember
that in moments of silence, with stilled hearts, we know that you are the true
God. Oftentimes we are so busy trying to catch up with our frantic schedules and
demands. Yet, we know Lord that we also need to stop and smell the flowers along
the way, to watch the sun set or to appreciate a lovely painting. We know we need to
give time to listen to our neighbors if we want to show love. We pray for peace and
serenity for the whole world which only your presence can give.*
Amen!.

DAY TWENTY-TWO

*Lord, you have always shown how important each of us is to you. You know all our
names and you love us with a true love that is focused alone on us. We humbly pray
that you show us the way to value and respect every person that crosses our lives.*
Amen!

DAY TWENTY-THREE

Lord, I pray for goodwill and peace for the whole world. I pray for the same goodwill and peace to transform my heart and make me a better person. I pray for peace and goodwill especially to people who have done me a wrong. Make me as generous to other people as you are with me. O God,
I know I have free will
To do actions
That can make the world feel a better place to live.
Yet, I still believe
It is only you who can
Guide me in the right path.
Help me Lord
As I try to bring
Peace and lightness to the world.
Help me start in small steps,
At work and at home,
To make a difference, and
to make it better for all people around me.
Grant me a patient heart
To understand
That it takes time
before something better happens.
Amen!

DAY TWENTY-FOUR

Lord, you alone
See how my heart sorrows,
For you alone love me best.
Hear my cry Lord
As I put my trust in you.
Live in my heart and mind
And lead me to a new life
filled with your spirit.
Amen!

DAY TWENTY-FIVE

Prayer for Christmas 1

Creator of all, God of love,
The darkness that has shrouded the earth
Has become brighter given by the
bright light of your promises.
Grant us to become
Followers of your light
As we follow your will
and shed your light to the whole world.
Amen!

Prayer for Christmas 2

O Lord,
This most holy of nights shine
Bright through your
true light illuminating the whole world.
We humbly beg you as we ask
That we will joyfully be with you in heaven as
You have revealed the reason for the light on earth.
Amen!

Prayer for Christmas 3

Lord, our hearts
Are filled with gladness
For this yearly celebration
Of the birth of Jesus Christ;
Make us become confident
To face Him in heaven
During judgment day
For we have joyfully followed His teachings.
Amen!

Prayer for Christmas 4

O God,
Wonderful creator, and
Wonderful restorer
Of the dignity of human souls,
Help us to become
As divine as Him
Who, in His love
For mankind,
humbly shared our humanity.
Amen!

DAY TWENTY-SIX

We pray O Lord for the young people who endure feelings of guilt and deep anxiety. We cannot imagine the pain they go through. Yet, we know that you love all of them even when most of them feel unappreciated. Help them to stop from seeking self harm. Help them to find a better way of letting go of their anxieties. Help them to find a way to express their anxieties in a healthy way. We know that you have taken steps to help them and for this we are very thankful.
Amen!

DAY TWENTY-SEVEN

Lord,
In a crowd are many faces,
With their own lives to lead,
With their own individual needs,
With their own dreams and phobias,
and with their own prayers and thoughts.
Some people do not want to be
just a face in the crowd,
some want to stand out from the rest.
Yet, I am aware,
That the greatest grace
Comes from just being
a true crowd member.
Lord, I ask for humility and wisdom
To remember that standing
Out from the rest of the crowd,
Will never compare to the
greater joy of sharing and working together.
Amen!

DAY TWENTY-EIGHT

I thank you Lord
For all the lovely blessings,
abundantly showered on me over the years.
The high and low times in my
life are all considered blessings to be thanked for.
Without your presence Lord,
Life will have no meaning,
Even when there are times
I ponder on the meaning of
the blessings that come my way.
Make me feel you love,
As I praise your Holy name.
Raise me up when I have doubts,
just as I am always thankful for the gift of salvation.
The moment we are born,
We are destined to live and die,
With our bodies becoming as dust,
Yet, we live because of your love
and your promise of salvation.
Make me a good servant as I show others
of your love for them.
Amen!

DAY TWENTY-NINE

Prayer for the Feast of the Holy Innocents

Lord, today,
We remember how
King Herod killed
In Bethlehem,
the holy innocents.
We pray,
That you cuddle
In your loving arms,
All innocent blood that are
tyrannized by evil people.
Give strength to fight off
This tyranny to
Build your kingdom of
Peace, justice, and love.
Amen!

DAY THIRTY

Lord, let me always be humble and generous towards my fellowmen. Grant in me a generous heart to accept people and never to discriminate against them. Inspire in me a life that is eager to discover the beauty in people and see you in them.
Amen!

DAY THIRTY-ONE

Prayer for the last day of the year 1

Lord, I thank you for giving me another opportunity to see the end of an old year. Great is your faithfulness O Lord. The past year has brought on sins and problems which seem to be my sole contribution. Yet, your forgiveness again and again has given me new hope to enjoy my life. Seasons in my life in the past year has brought on the warmness of summer, the brightness of spring, and the coldness of autumn and winter. Every good thing that has come to me came only from you Lord. Help me to remember to give value my days on earth with you as I look forward to another new year with you.

Amen!

Prayer for the last day of the year 2

Lord, your light has faithfully shone to me every day in the past years. I am so thankful for this. Thank you for the extension of another year in my life as I close the book of the past year. Thank you for the faithfulness of your presence even during the hard times when I needed you most. Give us strength and purpose to remain true and steadfast to you as we glorify your mighty name. You are our God and have saved us from our sins. You always fulfil your promises and we give thanks and praise to your Holy Name. We pray for other people to return to the fold and worship you.

Amen!

Prayer for the last day of the year 3

Lord, on this last day of the year, we humbly beg you to bless us again for the coming New Year. We pray that you touch the hearts of sinners to make them return to you. Grant peace and prosperity to our nation and to all the countries of the world. Bless our families, friends, and enemies. Give aid and comfort to the sick and poor. Be merciful to the souls of our beloved departed ones. Be merciful to the souls of people who will be called on their final journey this coming year. Make all our actions for the coming year in accordance to your will and not to our own.

Amen!

Prayer for the last day of the year 4

Lord, my mighty God and precious savior, I turn to you as another year unfolds. Lord some situations and problems have come on me the past year that will follow through on this New Year. I cry for help to you Lord. Give me wisdom and understanding through your Holy Spirit as I resolve these barriers. I am aware Lord that these trials come to make me learn to become a better person as befitting to the image of Jesus Christ.

Lord, make me remember that you will always be with me. Give rest to my troubled heart. Renew your promises to me this New Year. Help me and protect me from my enemies.

Remove disappointments and discouragements from me as I face another year. Help me to follow you this coming year.

Make me your servant Lord, not only in words, but in actions as well. Help me to meet the challenges of opportunities you give instead of ignoring them.

Lord, I rest on your love and faithfulness to take over my life as I journey on this New Year. Grant that my actions for the coming year prove my love and faithfulness to you.

Grant me a generous heart to love my neighbor as I love myself. Make me walk humbly as I serve, glorify, and love you. Let my actions rest on your will and for your glorification. Let my good works shine before men to make them praise your Holy Name.

Thank you Lord for the countless mercies you have shown to me in the past year. Thank you for the endless gifts of forgiveness and love. Help me to remember to always listen to your words.
Amen!

Prayer for the last day of the year 5

Our Great God, we ask your presence and guidance as we embark on another journey this New Year.
Our dreams and hopes are high even when we do not know what the New Year brings. We pray for your presence as we face things in the coming year. We are confident to face the incoming year through your love and faithfulness.
Amen!

CONCLUSION

Thank you for completing a year full of eternal blessings. Thank you for being a part of the God's beloved followers who don't start their day without uttering the name of their God, who don't end their day, unless they have praised their Lord even for a single moment during the day.

These prayers are very powerful in the sense that they contain all sorts of positive emotions, virtues, characteristic traits that you always wanted to be in your life. What is more beautiful than grabbing an opportunity to bring limitless positivity into all of your all 365 days of a year along with seeking God's pleasure at the same time?

You might have experienced that people who go on a "diet" lose weight and then gain it back again. Why does this happen? The only reason is that they go on a "diet" and not make the process of "consuming less energy than they should spend" a part of their lives. I am not here trying to sort of advertise for any of my weight loss book or something, but I am trying to tell you that most people become attracted towards our Lord for a short time due to some precipitating factor (failure, divorce, bad health). Then when the bad phase is over, we tend to forget our Lord who took us out of that phase.

Isn't this similar to going on a "diet"? So, this book should act as a reminder for you that whenever you feel a couple of days or weeks or even months passed without praising or thanking or even asking from your Lord, you have something to hold onto. You should immediately let all the Satans in your mind or elsewhere go drown in shame of failure by opening the corresponding month and day from this book and reading the prayer at once. I challenge you, all the negativity, all the bad things in your life will go away and you will miraculously experience a change, a change which even saints have longed for.

Finally, if you find this book helpful, pray for me too, who put his yearlong efforts in constructing the powerful prayers which will be accepted when you utter them from your heart (if you believe they will be). As, it is written in Bible, "*...whatever you ask for in prayer, believe that you have received it, and it will be yours*".

Amen!

If you want even more prayers, read Oliver Powell's *The 100 Most Powerful Morning Prayers Every Christian Needs to know.*

Now available on Amazon.com!

OLIVER POWELL

THE 100 MOST
POWERFUL
MORNING
PRAYERS
EVERY CHRISTIAN
NEEDS TO KNOW

Made in the USA
Monee, IL
25 July 2020